How We Think

John Dewey

HAWK PRESS

Published by

Hawk Press
4836/24, Ansari Road, Daryaganj
New Delhi – 110 002
Phones: 91-11-23278618, 91-11-43667199
E-mail: thehawkpress@gmail.com
www.thehawkpress.com

ISBN: 978-93-88318-35-8

CONTENTS

PREFACE

Our schools are troubled with a multiplication of studies, each in turn having its own multiplication of materials and principles. Our teachers find their tasks made heavier in that they have come to deal with pupils individually and not merely in mass. Unless these steps in advance are to end in distraction, some clew of unity, some principle that makes for simplification, must be found. This book represents the conviction that the needed steadying and centralizing factor is found in adopting as the end of endeavor that attitude of mind, that habit of thought, which we call scientific. This scientific attitude of mind might, conceivably, be quite irrelevant to teaching children and youth. But this book also represents the conviction that such is not the case; that the native and unspoiled attitude of childhood, marked by ardent curiosity, fertile imagination, and love of experimental inquiry, is near, very near, to the attitude of the scientific mind. If these pages assist any to appreciate this kinship and to consider seriously how its recognition in educational practice would make for individual happiness and the reduction of social waste, the book will amply have served its purpose.

It is hardly necessary to enumerate the authors to whom I am indebted. My fundamental indebtedness is to my wife, by whom the ideas of this book were inspired, and through whose work in connection with the Laboratory School, existing in Chicago between 1896 and 1903, the ideas attained such concreteness as comes from embodiment and testing in practice. It is a pleasure, also, to acknowledge indebtedness to the intelligence and sympathy of those who coöperated as teachers and supervisors in the conduct of that school, and especially to Mrs. Ella Flagg Young, then a colleague in the University, and now Superintendent of the Schools of Chicago.

NEW YORK CITY,
December, 1909.

PART ONE

The Problem of Training Thought

Chapter One

WHAT IS THOUGHT?

§ 1. Varied Senses of the Term

Four senses of thought, from the wider to the limited

No words are oftener on our lips than thinking and thought. So profuse and varied, indeed, is our use of these words that it is not easy to define just what we mean by them. The aim of this chapter is to find a single consistent meaning. Assistance may be had by considering some typical ways in which the terms are employed. In the first place thought is used broadly, not to say loosely. Everything that comes to mind, that "goes through our heads," is called a thought. To think of a thing is just to be conscious of it in any way whatsoever. Second, the term is restricted by excluding whatever is directly presented; we think (or think of) only such things as we do not directly see, hear, smell, or taste. Then, third, the meaning is further limited to beliefs that rest upon some kind of evidence or testimony. Of this third type, two kinds—or, rather, two degrees—must be discriminated. In some cases, a belief is accepted with slight or almost no attempt to state the grounds that support it. In other cases, the ground or basis for a belief is deliberately sought and its adequacy to support the belief examined. This process is called reflective thought; it alone is truly educative in value, and it forms, accordingly, the principal subject of this volume. We shall now briefly describe each of the four senses.

Chance and idle thinking

I. In its loosest sense, thinking signifies everything that, as we say, is "in our heads" or that "goes through our minds." He who offers "a penny for your thoughts" does not expect to drive any great bargain. In calling the objects of his demand thoughts, he does not intend to ascribe to them dignity, consecutiveness, or truth. Any idle fancy, trivial recollection, or flitting impression will satisfy his demand. Daydreaming, building of castles in the air, that loose flux of casual and disconnected material that floats through our minds in relaxed moments are, in this random sense, thinking. More of our waking life than we should care to admit, even to ourselves, is likely to be whiled away in this inconsequential trifling with idle fancy and unsubstantial hope.

Reflective thought is consecutive, not merely a sequence

In this sense, silly folk and dullards think. The story is told of a man in slight repute for intelligence, who, desiring to be chosen selectman in his New England town, addressed a knot of neighbors in this wise: "I hear you don't believe I know enough to hold office. I wish you to understand that I am thinking about something or other most of the time." Now reflective thought is like this random coursing of things through the mind in that it consists of a succession of things thought of; but it is unlike, in that the mere chance occurrence of any chance "something or other" in an irregular sequence does not suffice. Reflection involves not simply a sequence of ideas, but a consequence—a consecutive ordering in such a way that each determines the next as its proper outcome, while each in turn leans back on its predecessors. The successive portions of the reflective thought grow out of one another and support one another; they do not come and go in a medley. Each phase is a step from something to something—technically speaking, it is a term of thought. Each term leaves a deposit which is utilized in the next term. The stream or flow becomes a train, chain, or thread.

The restriction of thinking to what goes beyond direct observation

Reflective thought aims, however, at belief

II. Even when thinking is used in a broad sense, it is usually restricted to matters not directly perceived: to what we do not see, smell, hear, or touch. We ask the man telling a story if he saw a certain incident happen, and his reply may be, "No, I only thought of it." A note of invention, as distinct from faithful record of observation, is present. Most important in this class are successions of imaginative incidents and episodes which, having a certain coherence, hanging together on a continuous thread, lie between kaleidoscopic flights of fancy and considerations deliberately employed to establish a conclusion. The imaginative stories poured forth by children possess all degrees of internal congruity; some are disjointed, some are articulated. When connected, they simulate reflective thought; indeed, they usually occur in minds of logical capacity. These imaginative enterprises often precede thinking of the close-knit type and prepare the way for it. But they do not aim at knowledge, at belief about facts or in truths; and thereby they are marked off from reflective thought even when they most resemble it. Those who express such thoughts do not expect credence, but rather credit for a well-constructed plot or a well-arranged climax. They produce good stories, not—unless by chance—knowledge. Such thoughts are an efflorescence of feeling; the enhancement of a mood or sentiment is their aim; congruity of emotion, their binding tie.

Thought induces belief in two ways

III. In its next sense, thought denotes belief resting upon some basis, that is, real or supposed knowledge going beyond what is directly present. It is marked by acceptance or rejection of something as reasonably probable or improbable. This phase of thought, however, includes two such distinct types of belief that, even though their difference is strictly one of degree, not of kind, it becomes practically important to consider them separately. Some beliefs are accepted when their grounds have not themselves been considered, others are accepted because their grounds have been examined.

When we say, "Men used to think the world was flat," or, "I thought you went by the house," we express belief: something is accepted, held to, acquiesced in, or affirmed. But such thoughts may mean a supposition accepted without reference to its real grounds. These may be adequate, they may not; but their value with reference to the support they afford the belief has not been considered.

Such thoughts grow up unconsciously and without reference to the attainment of correct belief. They are picked up—we know not how. From obscure sources and by unnoticed channels they insinuate themselves into acceptance and become unconsciously a part of our mental furniture. Tradition, instruction, imitation—all of which depend upon authority in some form, or appeal to our own advantage, or fall in with a strong passion—are responsible for them. Such thoughts are prejudices, that is, prejudgments, not judgments proper that rest upon a survey of evidence.

Thinking in its best sense is that which considers the basis and consequences of beliefs

IV. Thoughts that result in belief have an importance attached to them which leads to reflective thought, to conscious inquiry into the nature, conditions, and bearings of the belief. To think of whales and camels in the clouds is to entertain ourselves with fancies, terminable at our pleasure, which do not lead to any belief in particular. But to think of the world as flat is to ascribe a quality to a real thing as its real property. This conclusion denotes a connection among things and hence is not, like imaginative thought, plastic to our mood. Belief in the world's flatness commits him who holds it to thinking in certain specific ways of other objects, such as the heavenly bodies, antipodes, the possibility of navigation. It prescribes to him actions in accordance with his conception of these objects.

The consequences of a belief upon other beliefs and upon behavior may be so important, then, that men are forced to consider the grounds or reasons of their belief and its logical consequences. This means reflective thought—thought in its eulogistic and emphatic sense.

Reflective thought defined

Men thought the world was flat until Columbus thought it to be round. The earlier thought was a belief held because men had not the energy or the courage to question what those about them accepted and taught, especially as it was suggested and seemingly confirmed by obvious sensible facts. The thought of Columbus was a reasoned conclusion. It marked the close of study into facts, of scrutiny and revision of evidence, of working out the implications of various hypotheses, and of comparing these theoretical results with one another and with known facts. Because Columbus did not accept unhesitatingly the current traditional theory, because he doubted and inquired, he arrived at his thought. Skeptical of what, from long habit, seemed most certain, and credulous of what seemed impossible, he went on thinking until he could produce evidence for both his confidence and his disbelief. Even if his conclusion had finally turned out wrong, it would have been a different sort of belief from those it antagonized, because it was reached by a different method. Active, persistent, and careful consideration of any belief or supposed form of knowledge in the light of the grounds that support it, and the further conclusions to which it tends, constitutes reflective thought. Any one of the first three kinds of thought may elicit this type; but once begun, it is a conscious and voluntary effort to establish belief upon a firm basis of reasons.

§ 2. The Central Factor in Thinking

There is a common element in all types of thought

There are, however, no sharp lines of demarcation between the various operations just outlined. The problem of attaining correct habits of reflection would be much easier than it is, did not the different modes of thinking blend insensibly into one another. So far, we have considered rather extreme instances of each kind in order to get the field clearly before us. Let us now reverse this operation; let us consider a rudimentary case of thinking, lying between careful examination of evidence and a mere irresponsible stream of fancies. A man is walking on a warm day. The sky was clear the last time he observed it; but presently he notes, while occupied primarily with other things, that the air is cooler. It occurs to him that it is probably going to rain; looking up, he sees a dark cloud between him and the sun, and he then quickens his steps. What, if anything, in such a situation can be called thought? Neither the act of walking nor the noting of the cold is a thought. Walking is one direction of activity; looking and noting are other modes of activity. The likelihood that it will rain is, however, something suggested. The pedestrian feels the cold; he thinks of clouds and a coming shower.

But reflection involves also the relation of signifying

So far there is the same sort of situation as when one looking at a cloud is reminded of a human figure and face. Thinking in both of these cases (the cases of belief and of fancy) involves a noted or perceived fact, followed by something else which is not observed but which is brought to mind, suggested by the thing seen. One reminds us, as we say, of the other. Side by side, however, with this factor of agreement in the two cases of suggestion is a factor of marked disagreement. We do not believe in the face suggested by the cloud; we do not consider at all the probability of its being a fact. There is no reflective thought. The danger of rain, on the contrary, presents itself to us as a genuine possibility—as a possible fact of the same nature as the observed coolness. Put differently, we do not regard the cloud as meaning or indicating a face, but merely as suggesting it, while we do consider that the coolness may mean rain. In the first case, seeing an object, we just happen, as we say, to think of something else; in the second, we consider the possibility and nature of the connection between the object seen and the object suggested. The seen thing is regarded as in some way the ground or basis of belief in the suggested thing; it possesses the quality of evidence.

Various synonymous expressions for the function of signifying

This function by which one thing signifies or indicates another, and thereby leads us to consider how far one may be regarded as warrant for belief in the other, is, then, the central factor in all reflective or distinctively intellectual thinking. By calling up various situations to which such terms as signifies and indicates apply, the student will best realize for himself the actual facts denoted by the words reflective thought. Synonyms for these terms are: points to, tells of, betokens, prognosticates, represents, stands for, implies. We also say one thing portends another; is ominous of another, or a symptom of it, or a key to it, or (if the connection is quite obscure) that it gives a hint, clue, or intimation.

Reflection and belief on evidence

Reflection thus implies that something is believed in (or disbelieved in), not on its own direct account, but through something else which stands as witness, evidence, proof, voucher, warrant; that is, as ground of belief. At one time, rain is actually felt or directly experienced; at another time, we infer that it has rained from the looks of the grass and trees, or that it is going to rain because of the condition of the air or the state of the barometer. At one time, we see a man (or suppose we do) without any intermediary fact; at another time, we are not quite sure what we see, and hunt for accompanying facts that will serve as signs, indications, tokens of what is to be believed.

Thinking, for the purposes of this inquiry, is defined accordingly as that operation in which present facts suggest other facts (or truths) in such a way as to induce belief in the latter upon the ground or warrant of the former. We do not put beliefs that rest simply on inference on the surest level of assurance. To say "I think so" implies that I do not as yet know so. The inferential belief may later be confirmed and come to stand as sure, but in itself it always has a certain element of supposition.

§ 3. Elements in Reflective Thinking

So much for the description of the more external and obvious aspects of the fact called thinking. Further consideration at once reveals certain subprocesses which are involved in every reflective operation. These are: (a) a state of perplexity, hesitation, doubt; and (b) an act of search or investigation directed toward bringing to light further facts which serve to corroborate or to nullify the suggested belief.

The importance of uncertainty

(a) In our illustration, the shock of coolness generated confusion and suspended belief, at least momentarily. Because it was unexpected, it was a shock or an interruption needing to be accounted for, identified, or placed. To say that the abrupt occurrence of the change of temperature constitutes a problem may sound forced and artificial; but if we are willing to extend the meaning of the word problem to whatever—no matter how slight and commonplace in character—perplexes and challenges the mind so that it makes belief at all uncertain, there is a genuine problem or question involved in this experience of sudden change.

(b) The turning of the head, the lifting of the eyes, the scanning of the heavens, are activities adapted to bring to recognition facts that will answer the question presented by the sudden coolness. The facts as they first presented themselves were perplexing; they suggested, however, clouds. The act of looking was an act to discover if this suggested explanation held good. It may again seem forced to speak of this looking, almost automatic, as an act of research or inquiry. But once more, if we are willing to generalize our conceptions of our mental operations to include the trivial and ordinary as well as the technical and recondite, there is no good reason for refusing to give such a title to the act of looking. The purport of this act of inquiry is to confirm or to refute the suggested belief. New facts are brought to perception, which either corroborate the idea that a change of weather is imminent, or negate it.

Finding one's way an illustration of reflection

Another instance, commonplace also, yet not quite so trivial, may enforce this lesson. A man traveling in an unfamiliar region comes to a branching of the roads. Having no sure knowledge to fall back upon, he is brought to a standstill of hesitation and suspense. Which road is right? And how shall perplexity be resolved? There are but two alternatives: he must either blindly and arbitrarily take his course, trusting to luck for the outcome, or he must discover grounds for the conclusion that a given road is right. Any attempt to decide the matter by thinking will involve inquiry into other facts, whether brought out by memory or by further observation, or by both. The perplexed wayfarer must carefully scrutinize what is before him and he must cudgel his memory. He looks for evidence that will support belief in favor of either of the roads—for evidence that will weight down one suggestion. He may climb a tree; he may go first in this direction, then in that, looking, in either case, for signs, clues, indications. He wants something in the nature of a signboard or a map, and his reflection is aimed at the discovery of facts that will serve this purpose.

Possible, yet incompatible, suggestions

The above illustration may be generalized. Thinking begins in what may fairly enough be called a forked-road situation, a situation which is ambiguous, which presents a dilemma, which proposes alternatives. As long as our activity glides smoothly along from one thing to another, or as long as we permit our imagination to entertain fancies at pleasure, there is no call for reflection. Difficulty or obstruction in the way of reaching a belief brings us, however, to a pause. In the suspense of uncertainty, we metaphorically climb a tree; we try to find some standpoint from which we may survey additional facts and, getting a more commanding view of the situation, may decide how the facts stand related to one another.

Regulation of thinking by its purpose

Demand for the solution of a perplexity is the steadying and guiding factor in the entire process of reflection. Where there is no question of a problem to be solved or a difficulty to be surmounted, the course of suggestions flows on at random; we have the first type of thought described. If the stream of suggestions is controlled simply by their emotional congruity, their fitting agreeably into a single picture or story, we have the second type. But a question to be answered, an ambiguity to be resolved, sets up an end and holds the current of ideas to a definite channel. Every suggested conclusion is tested by its reference to this regulating end, by its pertinence to the problem in hand. This need of straightening out a perplexity also controls the kind of inquiry undertaken. A traveler whose end is the most beautiful path will look for other considerations and will test suggestions occurring to him on another principle than if he wishes to discover the way to a given city. The problem fixes the end of thought and the end controls the process of thinking.

§ 4. Summary

Origin and stimulus

We may recapitulate by saying that the origin of thinking is some perplexity, confusion, or doubt. Thinking is not a case of spontaneous combustion; it does not occur just on "general principles." There is something specific which occasions and evokes it. General appeals to a child (or to a grown-up) to think, irrespective of the existence in his own experience of some difficulty that troubles him and disturbs his equilibrium, are as futile as advice to lift himself by his boot-straps.

Suggestions and past experience

Given a difficulty, the next step is suggestion of some way out—the formation of some tentative plan or project, the entertaining of some theory which will account for the peculiarities in question, the consideration of some solution for the problem. The data at hand cannot supply the solution; they can only suggest it. What, then, are the sources of the suggestion? Clearly past experience and prior knowledge. If the person has had some acquaintance with similar situations, if he has dealt with material of the same sort before, suggestions more or less apt and helpful are likely to arise. But unless there has been experience in some degree analogous, which may now be represented in imagination, confusion remains mere confusion. There is nothing upon which to draw in order to clarify it. Even when a child (or a grown-up) has a problem, to urge him to think when he has no prior experiences involving some of the same conditions, is wholly futile.

Exploration and testing

If the suggestion that occurs is at once accepted, we have uncritical thinking, the minimum of reflection. To turn the thing over in mind, to reflect, means to hunt for additional evidence, for new data, that will develop the suggestion, and will either, as we say, bear it out or else make obvious its absurdity and irrelevance. Given a genuine difficulty and a reasonable amount of analogous experience to draw upon, the difference, par excellence, between good and bad thinking is found at this point. The easiest way is to accept any suggestion that seems plausible and thereby bring to an end the condition of mental uneasiness. Reflective thinking is always more or less troublesome because it involves overcoming the inertia that inclines one to accept suggestions at their face value; it involves willingness to endure a condition of mental unrest and disturbance. Reflective thinking, in short, means judgment suspended during further inquiry; and suspense is likely to be somewhat painful. As we shall see later, the most important factor in the training of good mental habits consists in acquiring the attitude of suspended conclusion, and in mastering the various methods of searching for new materials to corroborate or to refute the first suggestions that occur. To maintain the state of doubt and to carry on systematic and protracted inquiry—these are the essentials of thinking.

Chapter Two

The Need For Training Thought

Man the animal that thinks

To expatiate upon the importance of thought would be absurd. The traditional definition of man as "the thinking animal" fixes thought as the essential difference between man and the brutes—surely an important matter. More relevant to our purpose is the question how thought is important, for an answer to this question will throw light upon the kind of training thought requires if it is to subserve its end.

§ 1. The Values of Thought

The possibility of deliberate and intentional activity

I. Thought affords the sole method of escape from purely impulsive or purely routine action. A being without capacity for thought is moved only by instincts and appetites, as these are called forth by outward conditions and by the inner state of the organism. A being thus moved is, as it were, pushed from behind. This is what we mean by the blind nature of brute actions. The agent does not see or foresee the end for which he is acting, nor the results produced by his behaving in one way rather than in another. He does not "know what he is about." Where there is thought, things present act as signs or tokens of things not yet experienced. A thinking being can, accordingly, act on the basis of the absent and the future. Instead of being pushed into a mode of action by the sheer urgency of forces, whether instincts or habits, of which he is not aware, a reflective agent is drawn (to some extent at least) to action by some remoter object of which he is indirectly aware.

Natural events come to be a language

An animal without thought may go into its hole when rain threatens, because of some immediate stimulus to its organism. A thinking agent will perceive that certain given facts are probable signs of a future rain, and will take steps in the light of this anticipated future. To plant seeds, to cultivate the soil, to harvest grain, are intentional acts, possible only to a being who has learned to subordinate the immediately felt elements of an experience to those values which these hint at and prophesy. Philosophers have made much of the phrases "book of nature," "language of nature." Well, it is in virtue of the capacity of thought that given things are significant of absent things, and that nature speaks a language which may be interpreted. To a being who thinks, things are records of their past, as fossils tell of the prior history of the earth, and are prophetic of their future, as from the present positions of heavenly bodies remote eclipses are foretold. Shakespeare's "tongues in trees, books in the running brooks," expresses literally enough the power superadded to existences when they appeal to a thinking being. Upon the function of signification depend all foresight, all intelligent planning, deliberation, and calculation.

The possibility of systematized foresight

II. By thought man also develops and arranges artificial signs to remind him in advance of consequences, and of ways of securing and avoiding them. As the trait just mentioned makes the difference between savage man and brute, so this trait makes the difference between civilized man and savage. A savage who has been shipwrecked in a river may note certain things which serve him as signs of danger in the future. But civilized man deliberately makes such signs; he sets up in advance of wreckage warning buoys, and builds lighthouses where he sees signs that such events may occur. A savage reads weather signs with great expertness; civilized man institutes a weather service by which signs are artificially secured and information is distributed in advance of the appearance of any signs that could be detected without special methods. A savage finds his way skillfully through a wilderness by reading certain obscure indications; civilized man builds a highway which shows the road to all. The savage learns to detect the signs of fire and thereby to invent methods of producing flame; civilized man invents permanent conditions for producing light and heat whenever they are needed. The very essence of civilized culture is that we deliberately erect monuments and memorials, lest we forget; and deliberately institute, in advance of the happening of various contingencies and emergencies of life, devices for detecting their approach and registering their nature, for warding off what is unfavorable, or at least for protecting ourselves from its full impact and for making more secure and extensive what is favorable. All forms of artificial apparatus are intentionally designed modifications of natural things in order that they may serve better than in their natural estate to indicate the hidden, the absent, and the remote.

The possibility of objects rich in quality

III. Finally, thought confers upon physical events and objects a very different status and value from that which they possess to a being that does not reflect. These words are mere scratches, curious variations of light and shade, to one to whom they are not linguistic signs. To him for whom they are signs of other things, each has a definite individuality of its own, according to the meaning that it is used to convey. Exactly the same holds of natural objects. A chair is a different object to a being to whom it consciously suggests an opportunity for sitting down, repose, or sociable converse, from what it is to one to whom it presents itself merely as a thing to be smelled, or gnawed, or jumped over; a stone is different to one who knows something of its past history and its future use from what it is to one who only feels it directly through his senses. It is only by courtesy, indeed, that we can say that an unthinking animal experiences an object at all—so largely is anything that presents itself to us as an object made up by the qualities it possesses as a sign of other things.

The nature of the objects an animal perceives

An English logician (Mr. Venn) has remarked that it may be questioned whether a dog sees a rainbow any more than he apprehends the political constitution of the country in which he lives. The same principle applies to the kennel in which he sleeps and the meat that he eats. When he is sleepy, he goes to the kennel; when he is hungry, he is excited by the smell and color of meat; beyond this, in what sense does he see an object? Certainly he does not see a house—i.e. a thing with all the properties and relations of a permanent residence, unless he is capable of making what is present a uniform sign of what is absent—unless he is capable of thought. Nor does he see what he eats as meat unless it suggests the absent properties by virtue of which it is a certain joint of some animal, and is known to afford nourishment. Just what is left of an object stripped of all such qualities of meaning, we cannot well say; but we can be sure that the object is then a very different sort of thing from the objects that we perceive. There[Pg 18] is moreover no particular limit to the possibilities of growth in the fusion of a thing as it is to sense and as it is to thought, or as a sign of other things. The child today soon regards as constituent parts of objects qualities that once it required the intelligence of a Copernicus or a Newton to apprehend.

Mill on the business of life and the occupation of mind

These various values of the power of thought may be summed up in the following quotation from John Stuart Mill. "To draw inferences," he says, "has been said to be the great business of life. Every one has daily, hourly, and momentary need of ascertaining facts which he has not directly observed: not from any general purpose of adding to his stock of knowledge, but because the facts themselves are of importance to his interests or to his occupations. The business of the magistrate, of the military commander, of the navigator, of the physician, of the agriculturist, is merely to judge of evidence and to act accordingly.... As they do this well or ill, so they discharge well or ill the duties of their several callings. It is the only occupation in which the mind never ceases to be engaged."

§ 2. Importance of Direction in order to Realize these Values

Thinking goes astray

What a person has not only daily and hourly, but momentary need of performing, is not a technical and abstruse matter; nor, on the other hand, is it trivial and negligible. Such a function must be congenial to the mind, and must be performed, in an unspoiled mind, upon every fitting occasion. Just because, however, it is an operation of drawing inferences, of basing conclusions upon evidence, of reaching belief indirectly, it is an operation that may go wrong as well as right, and hence is one that needs safeguarding and training. The greater its importance the greater are the evils when it is ill-exercised.

Ideas are our rulers—for better or for worse

An earlier writer than Mill, John Locke (1632-1704), brings out the importance of thought for life and the need of training so that its best and not its worst possibilities will be realized, in the following words: "No man ever sets himself about anything but upon some view or other, which serves him for a reason for what he does; and whatsoever faculties he employs, the understanding with such light as it has, well or ill informed, constantly leads; and by that light, true or false, all his operative powers are directed.... Temples have their sacred images, and we see what influence they have always had over a great part of mankind. But in truth the ideas and images in men's minds are the invisible powers that constantly govern them, and to these they all, universally, pay a ready submission. It is therefore of the highest concernment that great care should be taken of the understanding, to conduct it aright in the search of knowledge and in the judgments it makes." If upon thought hang all deliberate activities and the uses we make of all our other powers, Locke's assertion that it is of the highest concernment that care should be taken of its conduct is a moderate statement. While the power of thought frees us from servile subjection to instinct, appetite, and routine, it also brings with it the occasion and possibility of error and mistake. In elevating us above the brute, it opens to us the possibility of failures to which the animal, limited to instinct, cannot sink.

§ 3. Tendencies Needing Constant Regulation

Physical and social sanctions of correct thinking

Upto a certain point, the ordinary conditions of life, natural and social, provide the conditions requisite for regulating the operations of inference. The necessities of life enforce a fundamental and persistent discipline for which the most cunningly devised artifices would be ineffective substitutes. The burnt child dreads the fire; the painful consequence emphasizes the need of correct inference much more than would learned discourse on the properties of heat. Social conditions also put a premium on correct inferring in matters where action based on valid thought is socially important. These sanctions of proper thinking may affect life itself, or at least a life reasonably free from perpetual discomfort. The signs of enemies, of shelter, of food, of the main social conditions, have to be correctly apprehended.

The serious limitations of such sanctions

But this disciplinary training, efficacious as it is within certain limits, does not carry us beyond a restricted boundary. Logical attainment in one direction is no bar to extravagant conclusions in another. A savage expert in judging signs of the movements and location of animals that he hunts, will accept and gravely narrate the most preposterous yarns concerning the origin of their habits and structures. When there is no directly appreciable reaction of the inference upon the security and prosperity of life, there are no natural checks to the acceptance of wrong beliefs. Conclusions may be generated by a modicum of fact merely because the suggestions are vivid and interesting; a large accumulation of data may fail to suggest a proper conclusion because existing customs are averse to entertaining it. Independent of training, there is a "primitive credulity" which tends to make no distinction between what a trained mind calls fancy and that which it calls a reasonable conclusion. The face in the clouds is believed in as some sort of fact, merely because it is forcibly suggested. Natural intelligence is no barrier to the propagation of error, nor large but untrained experience to the accumulation of fixed false beliefs. Errors may support one another mutually and weave an ever larger and firmer fabric of misconception. Dreams, the positions of stars, the lines of the hand, may be regarded as valuable signs, and the fall of cards as an inevitable omen, while natural events of the most crucial significance go disregarded. Beliefs in portents of various kinds, now mere nook and cranny superstitions, were once universal. A long discipline in exact science was required for their conquest.

Superstition as natural a result as science

In the mere function of suggestion, there is no difference between the power of a column of mercury to portend rain, and that of the entrails of an animal or the flight of birds to foretell the fortunes of war. For all anybody can tell in advance, the spilling of salt is as likely to import bad luck as the bite of a mosquito to import malaria. Only systematic regulation of the conditions under which observations are made and severe discipline of the habits of entertaining suggestions can secure a decision that one type of belief is vicious and the other sound. The substitution of scientific for superstitious habits of inference has not been brought about by any improvement in the acuteness of the senses or in the natural workings of the function of suggestion. It is the result of regulation of the conditions under which observation and inference take place.

General causes of bad thinking: Bacon's "idols"

It is instructive to note some of the attempts that have been made to classify the main sources of error in reaching beliefs. Francis Bacon, for example, at the beginnings of modern scientific inquiry, enumerated four such classes, under the somewhat fantastic title of "idols", spectral forms that allure the mind into false paths. These he called the idols, or phantoms, of the (a) tribe, (b) the marketplace, (c) the cave or den, and (d) the theater; or, less metaphorically, (a) standing erroneous methods (or at least temptations to error) that have their roots in human nature generally; (b) those that come from intercourse and language; (c) those that are due to causes peculiar to a specific individual; and finally, (d) those that have their sources in the fashion or general current of a period. Classifying these causes of fallacious belief somewhat differently, we may say that two are intrinsic and two are extrinsic. Of the intrinsic, one is common to all men alike (such as the universal tendency to notice instances that corroborate a favorite belief more readily than those that contradict it), while the other resides in the specific temperament and habits of the given individual. Of the extrinsic, one proceeds from generic social conditions—like the tendency to suppose that there is a fact wherever there is a word, and no fact where there is no linguistic term—while the other proceeds from local and temporary social currents.

Locke's method of dealing with typical forms of wrong belief is less formal and may be more enlightening. We can hardly do better than quote his forcible and quaint language, when, enumerating different classes of men, he shows different ways in which thought goes wrong:

(a) dependence on others,

1. "The first is of those who seldom reason at all, but do and think according to the example of others, whether parents, neighbors, ministers, or who else they are pleased to make choice of to have an implicit faith in, for the saving of themselves the pains and troubles of thinking and examining for themselves."

(b) self-interest

2. "This kind is of those who put passion in the place of reason, and being resolved that shall govern their actions and arguments, neither use their own, nor hearken to other people's reason, any farther than it suits their humor, interest, or party."

(c) circumscribed experience

3. "The third sort is of those who readily and sincerely follow reason, but for want of having that which one may call large, sound, roundabout sense, have not a full view of all that relates to the question.... They converse but with one sort of men, they read but one sort of books, they will not come in the hearing but of one sort of notions.... They have a pretty traffic with known correspondents in some little creek ... but will not venture out into the great ocean of knowledge." Men of originally equal natural parts may finally arrive at very different stores of knowledge and truth, "when all the odds between them has been the different scope that has been given to their understandings to range in, for the gathering up of information and furnishing their heads with ideas and notions and observations, whereon to employ their mind."

In another portion of his writings, Locke states the same ideas in slightly different form.

Effect of dogmatic principles

1. "That which is inconsistent with our principles is so far from passing for probable with us that it will not be allowed possible. The reverence borne to these principles is so great, and their authority so paramount to all other, that the testimony, not only of other men, but the evidence of our own senses are often rejected, when they offer to vouch anything contrary to these established rules.... There is nothing more ordinary than children's receiving into their minds propositions ... from their parents, nurses, or those about them; which being insinuated in their unwary as well as unbiased understandings, and fastened by degrees, are at last (and this whether true or false) riveted there by long custom and education, beyond all possibility of being pulled out again. For men, when they are grown up, reflecting upon their opinions and finding those of this sort to be as ancient in their minds as their very memories, not having

observed their early insinuation, nor by what means they got them, they are apt to reverence them as sacred things, and not to suffer them to be profaned, touched, or questioned." They take them as standards "to be the great and unerring deciders of truth and falsehood, and the judges to which they are to appeal in all manner of controversies."

Of closed minds

2. "Secondly, next to these are men whose understandings are cast into a mold, and fashioned just to the size of a received hypothesis." Such men, Locke goes on to say, while not denying the existence of facts and evidence, cannot be convinced by the evidence that would decide them if their minds were not so closed by adherence to fixed belief.

Of strong passion

3. "Predominant Passions. Thirdly, probabilities which cross men's appetites and prevailing passions run the same fate. Let ever so much probability hang on one side of a covetous man's reasoning, and money on the other, it is easy to foresee which will outweigh. Earthly minds, like mud walls, resist the strongest batteries.

Of dependence upon authority of others

4. "Authority. The fourth and last wrong measure of probability I shall take notice of, and which keeps in ignorance or error more people than all the others together, is the giving up our assent to the common received opinions, either of our friends or party, neighborhood or country."

Causes of bad mental habits are social as well as inborn

Both Bacon and Locke make it evident that over and above the sources of misbelief that reside in the natural tendencies of the individual (like those toward hasty and too far-reaching conclusions), social conditions tend to instigate and confirm wrong habits of thinking by authority, by conscious instruction, and by the even more insidious half-conscious influences of language, imitation, sympathy, and suggestion. Education has accordingly not only to safeguard an individual against the besetting erroneous tendencies of his own mind—its rashness, presumption, and preference of what chimes with self-interest to objective evidence—but also to undermine and destroy the accumulated and self-perpetuating prejudices of long ages. When social life in general has become more reasonable, more imbued with rational conviction, and less moved by stiff authority and blind passion, educational agencies may be more positive and constructive than at present, for they will work in harmony with the educative influence exercised willy-nilly by other social surroundings upon an individual's habits of thought and belief. At present, the work of teaching must not only transform natural tendencies into trained habits of thought, but must also fortify the mind against irrational tendencies current in the social environment, and help displace erroneous habits already produced.

§ 4. Regulation Transforms Inference into Proof

A leap is involved in all thinking

Thinking is important because, as we have seen, it is that function in which given or ascertained facts stand for or indicate others which are not directly ascertained. But the process of reaching the absent from the present is peculiarly exposed to error; it is liable to be influenced by almost any number of unseen and unconsidered causes—past experience, received dogmas, the stirring of self-interest, the arousing of passion, sheer mental laziness, a social environment steeped in biased traditions or animated by false expectations, and so on. The exercise of thought is, in the literal sense of that word, inference; by it one thing carries us over to the idea of, and belief in, another thing. It involves a jump, a leap, a going beyond what is surely known to something else accepted on its warrant. Unless one is an idiot, one simply cannot help having all things and events suggest other things not actually present, nor can one help a tendency to believe in the latter on the basis of the former. The very inevitableness of the jump, the leap, to something unknown, only emphasizes the necessity of attention to the conditions under which it occurs so that the danger of a false step may be lessened and the probability of a right landing increased.

Hence, the need of regulation which, when adequate, makes proof

Such attention consists in regulation (1) of the conditions under which the function of suggestion takes place, and (2) of the conditions under which credence is yielded to the suggestions that occur. Inference controlled in these two ways (the study of which in detail constitutes one of the chief objects of this book) forms proof. To prove a thing means primarily to try, to test it. The guest bidden to the wedding feast excused himself because he had to prove his oxen. Exceptions are said to prove a rule; i.e. they furnish instances so extreme that they try in the severest fashion its applicability; if the rule will stand such a test, there is no good reason for further doubting it. Not until a thing has been tried—"tried out," in colloquial language—do we know its true worth. Till then it may be pretense, a bluff. But the thing that has come out victorious in a test or trial of strength carries its credentials with it; it is approved, because it has been proved. Its value is clearly evinced, shown, i.e. demonstrated. So it is with inferences. The mere fact that inference in general is an invaluable function does not guarantee, nor does it even help out the correctness of any particular inference. Any inference may go astray; and as we have seen, there are standing influences ever ready to assist its going wrong. What is important, is that every inference shall be a tested inference; or (since often this is not possible) that we shall discriminate between beliefs that rest upon tested evidence and those that do not, and shall be accordingly on our guard as to the kind and degree of assent yielded.

The office of education in forming skilled powers of thinking

While it is not the business of education to prove every statement made, any more than to teach every possible item of information, it is its business to cultivate deep-seated and effective habits of discriminating tested beliefs from mere assertions, guesses, and opinions; to develop a lively, sincere, and open-minded preference for conclusions that are properly grounded, and to ingrain into the individual's working habits methods of inquiry and reasoning appropriate to the various problems that present themselves. No matter how much an individual knows as a matter of hearsay and information, if he has not attitudes and habits of this sort, he is not intellectually educated. He lacks the rudiments of mental discipline. And since these habits are not a gift of nature (no matter how strong the aptitude for acquiring them); since, moreover, the casual circumstances of the natural and social environment are not enough to compel their acquisition, the main office of education is to supply conditions that make for their cultivation. The formation of these habits is the Training of Mind.

Chapter Three

NATURAL RESOURCES IN THE TRAINING OF THOUGHT

Only native powers can be trained

In the last chapter we considered the need of transforming, through training, the natural capacities of inference into habits of critical examination and inquiry. The very importance of thought for life makes necessary its control by education because of its natural tendency to go astray, and because social influences exist that tend to form habits of thought leading to inadequate and erroneous beliefs. Training must, however, be itself based upon the natural tendencies—that is, it must find its point of departure in them. A being who could not think without training could never be trained to think; one may have to learn to think well, but not to think. Training, in short, must fall back upon the prior and independent existence of natural powers; it is concerned with their proper direction, not with creating them.

Hence, the one taught must take the initiative

Teaching and learning are correlative or corresponding processes, as much so as selling and buying. One might as well say he has sold when no one has bought, as to say that he has taught when no one has learned. And in the educational transaction, the initiative lies with the learner even more than in commerce it lies with the buyer. If an individual can learn to think only in the sense of learning to employ more economically and effectively powers he already possesses, even more truly one can teach others to think only in the sense of appealing to and fostering powers already active in them. Effective appeal of this kind is impossible unless the teacher has an insight into existing habits and tendencies, the natural resources with which he has to ally himself.

Three important natural resources

Any inventory of the items of this natural capital is somewhat arbitrary because it must pass over many of the complex details. But a statement of the factors essential to thought will put before us in outline the main elements. Thinking involves (as we have seen) the suggestion of a conclusion for acceptance, and also search or inquiry to test the value of the suggestion before finally accepting it. This implies (a) a certain fund or store of experiences and facts from which suggestions proceed; (b) promptness, flexibility, and fertility of suggestions; and (c) orderliness, consecutiveness, appropriateness in what is suggested. Clearly, a person may be hampered in any of these three regards: His thinking may be irrelevant, narrow, or crude because he has not enough actual material upon which to base conclusions; or because concrete facts and raw material, even if extensive and bulky, fail to evoke suggestions easily and richly; or finally, because, even when these two conditions are fulfilled, the ideas suggested are incoherent and fantastic, rather than pertinent and consistent.

§ 1. Curiosity

Desire for fullness of experience

The most vital and significant factor in supplying the primary material whence suggestion may issue is, without doubt, curiosity. The wisest of the Greeks used to say that wonder is the mother of all science. An inert mind waits, as it were, for experiences to be imperiously forced upon it. The pregnant saying of Wordsworth:

"The eye—it cannot choose but see;
We cannot bid the ear be still;
Our bodies feel, where'er they be,
Against or with our will"—

holds good in the degree in which one is naturally possessed by curiosity. The curious mind is constantly alert and exploring, seeking material for thought, as a vigorous and healthy body is on the *qui vive* for nutriment. Eagerness for experience, for new and varied contacts, is found where wonder is found. Such curiosity is the only sure guarantee of the acquisition of the primary facts upon which inference must base itself.

(a) Physical

(a) In its first manifestations, curiosity is a vital overflow, an expression of an abundant organic energy. A physiological uneasiness leads a child to be "into everything"—to be reaching, poking, pounding, prying. Observers of animals have noted what one author calls "their inveterate tendency to fool." "Rats run about, smell, dig, or gnaw, without real reference to the business in hand. In the same way Jack [a dog] scrabbles and jumps, the kitten wanders and picks, the otter slips about everywhere like ground lightning, the elephant fumbles ceaselessly, the monkey pulls things about." The most casual notice of the activities of a young child reveals a ceaseless display of exploring and testing activity. Objects are sucked, fingered, and thumped; drawn and pushed, handled and thrown; in short, experimented with, till they cease to yield new qualities. Such activities are hardly intellectual, and yet without them intellectual activity would be feeble and intermittent through lack of stuff for its operations.

(b) Social

(b) A higher stage of curiosity develops under the influence of social stimuli. When the child learns that he can appeal to others to eke out his store of experiences, so that, if objects fail to respond interestingly to his experiments, he may call upon persons to provide interesting material, a new epoch sets in. "What is that?" "Why?" become the unfailing signs of a child's presence. At first this questioning is hardly more than a projection into social relations of the physical overflow which earlier kept the child pushing and pulling, opening and shutting. He asks in succession what holds up the house, what holds up the soil that holds the house, what holds up the earth that holds the soil; but his questions are not evidence of any genuine consciousness of rational connections. His why is not a demand for scientific explanation; the motive behind it is simply eagerness for a larger acquaintance with the mysterious world in which he is placed. The search is not for a law or principle, but only for a bigger fact. Yet there is more than a desire to accumulate just information or heap up disconnected items, although sometimes the interrogating habit threatens to degenerate into a mere disease of language. In the feeling, however dim, that the facts which directly meet the senses are not the whole story, that there is more behind them and more to come from them, lies the germ of intellectual curiosity.

(c) Intellectual

(c) Curiosity rises above the organic and the social planes and becomes intellectual in the degree in which it is transformed into interest in problems provoked by the observation of things and the accumulation of material. When the question is not discharged by being asked of another, when the child continues to entertain it in his own mind and to be alert for whatever will help answer it, curiosity has become a positive intellectual force. To the open mind, nature and social experience are full of varied and subtle challenges to look further. If germinating powers are not used and cultivated at the right moment, they tend to be transitory, to die out, or to wane in intensity. This general law is peculiarly true of sensitiveness to what is uncertain and questionable; in a few people, intellectual curiosity is so insatiable that nothing will discourage it, but in most its edge is easily dulled and blunted. Bacon's saying that we must become as little children in order to enter the kingdom of science is at once a reminder of the open-minded and flexible wonder of childhood and of the ease with which this endowment is lost. Some lose it in indifference or carelessness; others in a frivolous flippancy; many escape these evils only to become incased in a hard dogmatism which is equally fatal to the spirit of wonder. Some are so taken up with routine as to be inaccessible to new facts and problems. Others retain curiosity only with reference to what concerns their personal advantage in their chosen career. With many, curiosity is arrested on the plane of interest in local gossip and in the fortunes of their neighbors; indeed, so usual is this result that very often the first association with the word curiosity is a prying inquisitiveness into other people's business. With respect then to curiosity, the teacher has usually more to learn than to teach. Rarely can he aspire to the office of kindling or even increasing it. His task is rather to keep alive the sacred spark of wonder and to fan the flame that already glows. His problem is to protect the spirit of inquiry, to keep it from becoming blasé from overexcitement, wooden from routine, fossilized through dogmatic instruction, or dissipated by random exercise upon trivial things.

§ 2. Suggestion

Out of the subject-matter, whether rich or scanty, important or trivial, of present experience issue suggestions, ideas, beliefs as to what is not yet given. The function of suggestion is not one that can be produced by teaching; while it may be modified for better or worse by conditions, it cannot be destroyed. Many a child has tried his best to see if he could not "stop thinking," but the flow of suggestions goes on in spite of our will, quite as surely as "our bodies feel, where'er they be, against or with our will." Primarily, naturally, it is not we who think, in any actively responsible sense; thinking is rather something that happens in us. Only so far as one has acquired control of the method in which the function of suggestion occurs and has accepted responsibility for its consequences, can one truthfully say, "I think so and so."

The dimensions of suggestion:

(a) ease

The function of suggestion has a variety of aspects (or dimensions as we may term them), varying in different persons, both in themselves and in their mode of combination. These dimensions are ease or promptness, extent or variety, and depth or persistence. (a) The common classification of persons into the dull and the bright is made primarily on the basis of the readiness or facility with which suggestions follow upon the presentation of objects and upon the happening of events. As the metaphor of dull and bright implies, some minds are impervious, or else they absorb passively. Everything presented is lost in a drab monotony that gives nothing back. But others reflect, or give back in varied lights, all that strikes upon them. The dull make no response; the bright flash back the fact with a changed quality. An inert or stupid mind requires a heavy jolt or an intense shock to move it to suggestion; the bright mind is quick, is alert to react with interpretation and suggestion of consequences to follow.

Yet the teacher is not entitled to assume stupidity or even dullness merely because of irresponsiveness to school subjects or to a lesson as presented by text-book or teacher. The pupil labeled hopeless may react in quick and lively fashion when the thing-in-hand seems to him worth while, as some out-of-school sport or social affair. Indeed, the school subject might move him, were it set in a different context and treated by a different method. A boy dull in geometry may prove quick enough when he takes up the subject in connection with manual training; the girl who seems inaccessible to historical facts may respond promptly when it is a question of judging the character and deeds of people of her acquaintance or of fiction. Barring physical defect or disease, slowness and dullness in all directions are comparatively rare.

(b) range

(b) Irrespective of the difference in persons as to the ease and promptness with which ideas respond to facts, there is a difference in the number or range of the suggestions that occur. We speak truly, in some cases, of the flood of suggestions; in others, there is but a slender trickle. Occasionally, slowness of outward response is due to a great variety of suggestions which check one another and lead to hesitation and suspense; while a lively and prompt suggestion may take such possession of the mind as to preclude the development of others. Too few suggestions indicate a dry and meager mental habit; when this is joined to great learning, there results a pedant or a Gradgrind. Such a person's mind rings hard; he is likely to bore others with mere bulk of information. He contrasts with the person whom we call ripe, juicy, and mellow.

A conclusion reached after consideration of a few alternatives may be formally correct, but it will not possess the fullness and richness of meaning of one arrived at after comparison of a greater variety of alternative suggestions. On the other hand, suggestions may be too numerous and too varied for the best interests of mental habit. So many suggestions may rise that the person is at a loss to select among them. He finds it difficult to reach any definite conclusion and wanders more or less helplessly among them. So much suggests itself pro and con, one thing leads on to another so naturally, that he finds it difficult to decide in practical affairs or to conclude in matters of theory. There is such a thing as too much thinking, as when action is paralyzed by the multiplicity of views suggested by a situation. Or again, the very number of suggestions may be hostile to tracing logical sequences among them, for it may tempt the mind away from the necessary but trying task of search for real connections, into the more congenial occupation of embroidering upon the given facts a tissue of agreeable fancies. The best mental habit involves a balance between paucity and redundancy of suggestions.

(c) profundity

(c) Depth. We distinguish between people not only upon the basis of their quickness and fertility of intellectual response, but also with respect to the plane upon which it occurs—the intrinsic quality of the response.

One man's thought is profound while another's is superficial; one goes to the roots of the matter, and another touches lightly its most external aspects. This phase of thinking is perhaps the most untaught of all, and the least amenable to external influence whether for improvement or harm. Nevertheless, the conditions of the pupil's contact with subject-matter may be such that he is compelled to come to quarters with its more significant features, or such that he is encouraged to deal with it upon the basis of what is trivial. The common assumptions that, if the pupil only thinks, one thought is just as good for his mental discipline as another, and that the end of study is the amassing of information, both tend to foster superficial, at the expense of significant, thought. Pupils who in matters of ordinary practical experience have a ready and acute perception of the difference between the significant and the meaningless, often reach in school subjects a point where all things seem equally important or equally unimportant; where one thing is just as likely to be true as another, and where intellectual effort is expended not in discriminating between things, but in trying to make verbal connections among words.

Balance of mind

Sometimes slowness and depth of response are intimately connected. Time is required in order to digest impressions, and translate them into substantial ideas. "Brightness" may be but a flash in the pan. The "slow but sure" person, whether man or child, is one in whom impressions sink and accumulate, so that thinking is done at a deeper level of value than with a slighter load. Many a child is rebuked for "slowness," for not "answering promptly," when his forces are taking time to gather themselves together to deal effectively with the problem at hand. In such cases, failure to afford time and leisure conduce to habits of speedy, but snapshot and superficial, judgment. The depth to which a sense of the problem, of the difficulty, sinks, determines the quality of the thinking that follows; and any habit of teaching which encourages the pupil for the sake of a successful recitation or of a display of memorized information to glide over the thin ice of genuine problems reverses the true method of mind training.

Individual differences

It is profitable to study the lives of men and women who achieve in adult life fine things in their respective callings, but who were called dull in their school days. Sometimes the early wrong judgment was due mainly to the fact that the direction in which the child showed his ability was not one recognized by the good old standards in use, as in the case of Darwin's interest in beetles, snakes, and frogs. Sometimes it was due to the fact that the child dwelling habitually on a deeper plane of reflection than other pupils—or than his teachers—did not show to advantage when prompt answers of the usual sort were expected. Sometimes it was due to the fact that the pupil's natural mode of approach clashed habitually with that of the text or teacher, and the method of the latter was assumed as an absolute basis of estimate.

Any subject may be intellectual

In any event, it is desirable that the teacher should rid himself of the notion that "thinking" is a single, unalterable faculty; that he should recognize that it is a term denoting the various ways in which things acquire significance. It is desirable to expel also the kindred notion that some subjects are inherently "intellectual," and hence possessed of an almost magical power to train the faculty of thought. Thinking is specific, not a machine-like, ready-made apparatus to be turned indifferently and at will upon all subjects, as a lantern may throw its light as it happens upon horses, streets, gardens, trees, or river. Thinking is specific, in that different things suggest their own appropriate meanings, tell their own unique stories, and in that they do this in very different ways with different persons. As the growth of the body is through the assimilation of food, so the growth of mind is through the logical organization of subject-matter. Thinking is not like a sausage machine which reduces all materials indifferently to one marketable commodity, but is a power of following up and linking together the specific suggestions that specific things arouse. Accordingly, any subject, from Greek to cooking, and from drawing to mathematics, is intellectual, if intellectual at all, not in its fixed inner structure, but in its function—in its power to start and direct significant inquiry and reflection. What geometry does for one, the manipulation of laboratory apparatus, the mastery of a musical composition, or the conduct of a business affair, may do for another.

§ 3. Orderliness: Its Nature

Continuity

Facts, whether narrow or extensive, and conclusions suggested by them, whether many or few, do not constitute, even when combined, reflective thought. The suggestions must be organized; they must be arranged with reference to one another and with reference to the facts on which they depend for proof. When the factors of facility, of fertility, and of depth are properly balanced or proportioned, we get as the outcome continuity of thought. We desire neither the slow mind nor yet the hasty. We wish neither random diffuseness nor fixed rigidity. Consecutiveness means flexibility and variety of materials, conjoined with singleness and definiteness of direction. It is opposed both to a mechanical routine uniformity and to a grasshopper-like movement. Of bright children, it is not infrequently said that "they might do anything, if only they settled down," so quick and apt are they in any particular response. But, alas, they rarely settle.

On the other hand, it is not enough not to be diverted. A deadly and fanatic consistency is not our goal. Concentration does not mean fixity, nor a cramped arrest or paralysis of the flow of suggestion. It means variety and change of ideas combined into a single steady trend moving toward a unified conclusion. Thoughts are concentrated not by being kept still and quiescent, but by being kept moving toward an object, as a general concentrates his troops for attack or defense. Holding the mind to a subject is like holding a ship to its course; it implies constant change of place combined with unity of direction. Consistent and orderly thinking is precisely such a change of subject-matter. Consistency is no more the mere absence of contradiction than concentration is the mere absence of diversion—which exists in dull routine or in a person "fast asleep." All kinds of varied and incompatible suggestions may sprout and be followed in their growth, and yet thinking be consistent and orderly, provided each one of the suggestions is viewed in relation to the main topic.

Practical demands enforce some degree of continuity

In the main, for most persons, the primary resource in the development of orderly habits of thought is indirect, not direct. Intellectual organization originates and for a time grows as an accompaniment of the organization of the acts required to realize an end, not as the result of a direct appeal to thinking power. The need of thinking to accomplish something beyond thinking is more potent than thinking for its own sake. All people at the outset, and the majority of people probably all their lives, attain ordering of thought through ordering of action. Adults normally carry on some occupation, profession, pursuit; and this furnishes the continuous axis about which their knowledge, their beliefs, and their habits of reaching and testing conclusions are organized. Observations that have to do with the efficient performance of their calling are extended and rendered precise. Information related to it is not merely amassed and then left in a heap; it is classified and subdivided so as to be available as it is needed. Inferences are made by most men not from purely speculative motives, but because they are involved in the efficient performance of "the duties involved in their several callings." Thus their inferences are constantly tested by results achieved; futile and scattering methods tend to be discounted; orderly arrangements have a premium put upon them. The event, the issue, stands as a constant check on the thinking that has led up to it; and this discipline by efficiency in action is the chief sanction, in practically all who are not scientific specialists, of orderliness of thought.

Such a resource—the main prop of disciplined thinking in adult life—is not to be despised in training the young in right intellectual habits. There are, however, profound differences between the immature and the adult in the matter of organized activity—differences which must be taken seriously into account in any educational use of activities: (i) The external achievement resulting from activity is a more urgent necessity with the adult, and hence is with him a more effective means of discipline of mind than with the child; (ii) The ends of adult activity are more specialized than those of child activity.

Peculiar difficulty with children

(i) The selection and arrangement of appropriate lines of action is a much more difficult problem as respects youth than it is in the case of adults. With the latter, the main lines are more or less settled by circumstances. The social status of the adult, the fact that he is a citizen, a householder, a parent, one occupied in some regular industrial or professional calling, prescribes the chief features of the acts to be performed, and secures, somewhat automatically, as it were, appropriate and related modes of thinking. But with the child there is no such fixity of status and pursuit; there is almost nothing to dictate that such and such a consecutive line of action, rather than another, should be followed, while the will of others, his own caprice, and circumstances about him tend to produce an isolated momentary act. The absence of continued motivation coöperates with the inner plasticity of the immature to increase the importance of educational training and the difficulties in the way of finding consecutive modes of activities which may do for child and youth what serious vocations and functions do for the adult. In the case of children, the choice is so peculiarly exposed to arbitrary factors, to mere school traditions, to waves of pedagogical fad and fancy, to fluctuating social cross currents, that sometimes, in sheer disgust at the inadequacy of results, a reaction occurs to the total neglect of overt activity as an educational factor, and a recourse to purely theoretical subjects and methods.

Peculiar opportunity with children

(ii) This very difficulty, however, points to the fact that the opportunity for selecting truly educative activities is indefinitely greater in child life than in adult. The factor of external pressure is so strong with most adults that the educative value of the pursuit—its reflex influence upon intelligence and character—however genuine, is incidental, and frequently almost accidental. The problem and the opportunity with the young is selection of orderly and continuous modes of occupation, which, while they lead up to and prepare for the indispensable activities of adult life, have their own sufficient justification in their present reflex influence upon the formation of habits of thought.

Action and reaction between extremes

Educational practice shows a continual tendency to oscillate between two extremes with respect to overt and exertive activities. One extreme is to neglect them almost entirely, on the ground that they are chaotic and fluctuating, mere diversions appealing to the transitory unformed taste and caprice of immature minds; or if they avoid this evil, are objectionable copies of the highly specialized, and more or less commercial, activities of adult life. If activities are admitted at all into the school, the admission is a grudging concession to the necessity of having occasional relief from the strain of constant intellectual work, or to the clamor of outside utilitarian demands upon the school. The other extreme is an enthusiastic belief in the almost magical educative efficacy of any kind of activity, granted it is an activity and not a passive absorption of academic and theoretic material. The conceptions of play, of self-expression, of natural growth, are appealed to almost as if they meant that opportunity for any kind of spontaneous activity inevitably secures the due training of mental power; or a mythological brain physiology is appealed to as proof that any exercise of the muscles trains power of thought.

Locating the problem of education

While we vibrate from one of these extremes to the other, the most serious of all problems is ignored: the problem, namely, of discovering and arranging the forms of activity (a) which are most congenial, best adapted, to the immature stage of development; (b) which have the most ulterior promise as preparation for the social responsibilities of adult life; and (c) which, at the same time, have the maximum of influence in forming habits of acute observation and of consecutive inference. As curiosity is related to the acquisition of material of thought, as suggestion is related to flexibility and force of thought, so the ordering of activities, not themselves primarily intellectual, is related to the forming of intellectual powers of consecutiveness.

Chapter Four

School Conditions and The Training of Thought

§ 1. Introductory: Methods and Conditions

Formal discipline

The so-called faculty-psychology went hand in hand with the vogue of the formal-discipline idea in education. If thought is a distinct piece of mental machinery, separate from observation, memory, imagination, and common-sense judgments of persons and things, then thought should be trained by special exercises designed for the purpose, as one might devise special exercises for developing the biceps muscles. Certain subjects are then to be regarded as intellectual or logical subjects par excellence, possessed of a predestined fitness to exercise the thought-faculty, just as certain machines are better than others for developing arm power. With these three notions goes the fourth, that method consists of a set of operations by which the machinery of thought is set going and kept at work upon any subject-matter.

Versus real thinking

We have tried to make it clear in the previous chapters that there is no single and uniform power of thought, but a multitude of different ways in which specific things—things observed, remembered, heard of, read about—evoke suggestions or ideas that are pertinent to the occasion and fruitful in the sequel. Training is such development of curiosity, suggestion, and habits of exploring and testing, as increases their scope and efficiency. A subject—any subject—is intellectual in the degree in which with any given person it succeeds in effecting this growth. On this view the fourth factor, method, is concerned with providing conditions so adapted to individual needs and powers as to make for the permanent improvement of observation, suggestion, and investigation.

True and false meaning of method

The teacher's problem is thus twofold. On the one side, he needs (as we saw in the last chapter) to be a student of individual traits and habits; on the other side, he needs to be a student of the conditions that modify for better or worse the directions in which individual powers habitually express themselves. He needs to recognize that method covers not only what he intentionally devises and employs for the purpose of mental training, but also what he does without any conscious reference to it—anything in the atmosphere and conduct of the school which reacts in any way upon the curiosity, the responsiveness, and the orderly activity of children. The teacher who is an intelligent student both of individual mental operations and of the effects of school conditions upon those operations, can largely be trusted to develop for himself methods of instruction in their narrower and more technical sense—those best adapted to achieve results in particular subjects, such as reading, geography, or algebra. In the hands of one who is not intelligently aware of individual capacities and of the influence unconsciously exerted upon them by the entire environment, even the best of technical methods are likely to get an immediate result only at the expense of deep-seated and persistent habits. We may group the conditioning influences of the school environment under three heads: (1) the mental attitudes and habits of thepersons with whom the child is in contact; (2) the subjects studied; (3) current educational aims and ideals.

§ 2. Influence of the Habits of Others

Bare reference to the imitativeness of human nature is enough to suggest how profoundly the mental habits of others affect the attitude of the one being trained. Example is more potent than precept; and a teacher's best conscious efforts may be more than counteracted by the influence of personal traits which he is unaware of or regards as unimportant. Methods of instruction and discipline that are technically faulty may be rendered practically innocuous by the inspiration of the personal method that lies back of them.

Response to environment fundamental in method

To confine, however, the conditioning influence of the educator, whether parent or teacher, to imitation is to get a very superficial view of the intellectual influence of others. Imitation is but one case of a deeper principle—that of stimulus and response. Everything the teacher does, as well as the manner in which he does it, incites the child to respond in some way or other, and each response tends to set the child's attitude in some way or other. Even the inattention of the child to the adult is often a mode of response which is the result of unconscious training. The teacher is rarely (and even then never entirely) a transparent medium of access by another mind to a subject. With the young, the influence of the teacher's personality is intimately fused with that of the subject; the child does not separate nor even distinguish the two. And as the child's response is toward or away from anything presented, he keeps up a running commentary, of which he himself is hardly distinctly aware, of like and dislike, of sympathy and aversion, not merely to the acts of the teacher, but also to the subject with which the teacher is occupied.

Influence of teacher's own habits

Judging others by ourselves

The extent and power of this influence upon morals and manners, upon character, upon habits of speech and social bearing, are almost universally recognized. But the tendency to conceive of thought as an isolated faculty has often blinded teachers to the fact that this influence is just as real and pervasive in intellectual concerns. Teachers, as well as children, stick more or less to the main points, have more or less wooden and rigid methods of response, and display more or less intellectual curiosity about matters that come up. And every trait of this kind is an inevitable part of the teacher's method of teaching. Merely to accept without notice slipshod habits of speech, slovenly inferences, unimaginative and literal response, is to indorse these tendencies, and to ratify them into habits—and so it goes throughout the whole range of contact between teacher and student. In this complex and intricate field, two or three points may well be singled out for special notice. (a) Most persons are quite unaware of the distinguishing peculiarities of their own mental habit. They take their own mental operations for granted, and unconsciously make them the standard for judging the mental processes of others. Hence there is a tendency to encourage everything in the pupil which agrees with this attitude, and to neglect or fail to understand whatever is incongruous with it. The prevalent overestimation of the value, for mind-training, of theoretic subjects as compared with practical pursuits, is doubtless due partly to the fact that the teacher's calling tends to select those in whom the theoretic interest is specially strong and to repel those in whom executive abilities are marked. Teachers sifted out on this basis judge pupils and subjects by a like standard, encouraging an intellectual one-sidedness in those to whom it is naturally congenial, and repelling from study those in whom practical instincts are more urgent.

Exaggeration of direct personal influence

(b) Teachers—and this holds especially of the stronger and better teachers—tend to rely upon their personal strong points to hold a child to his work, and thereby to substitute their personal influence for that of subject-matter as a motive for study. The teacher finds by experience that his own personality is often effective where the power of the subject to command attention is almost nil; then he utilizes the former more and more, until the pupil's relation to the teacher almost takes the place of his relation to the subject. In this way the teacher's personality may become a source of personal dependence and weakness, an influence that renders the pupil indifferent to the value of the subject for its own sake.

Independent thinking versus "getting the answer"

(c) The operation of the teacher's own mental habit tends, unless carefully watched and guided, to make the child a student of the teacher's peculiarities rather than of the subjects that he is supposed to study. His chief concern is to accommodate himself to what the teacher expects of him, rather than to devote himself energetically to the problems of subject-matter. "Is this right?" comes to mean "Will this answer or this process satisfy the teacher?"—instead of meaning, "Does it satisfy the inherent conditions of the problem?" It would be folly to deny the legitimacy or the value of the study of human nature that children carry on in school; but it is obviously undesirable that their chief intellectual problem should be that of producing an answer approved by the teacher, and their standard of success be successful adaptation to the requirements of another.

§ 3. Influence of the Nature of Studies

Types of studies

Studies are conventionally and conveniently grouped under these heads: (1) Those especially involving the acquisition of skill in performance— the school arts, such as reading, writing, figuring, and music. (2) Those mainly concerned with acquiring knowledge— "informational" studies, such as geography and history. (3) Those in which skill in doing and bulk of information are relatively less important, and appeal to abstract thinking, to "reasoning," is most marked—"disciplinary" studies, such as arithmetic and formal grammar. Each of these groups of subjects has its own special pitfalls.

The abstract as the isolated

(a) In the case of the so-called disciplinary or pre-eminently logical studies, there is danger of the isolation of intellectual activity from the ordinary affairs of life. Teacher and student alike tend to set up a chasm between logical thought as something abstract and remote, and the specific and concrete demands of everyday events. The abstract tends to become so aloof, so far away from application, as to be cut loose from practical and moral bearing. The gullibility of specialized scholars when out of their own lines, their extravagant habits of inference and speech, their ineptness in reaching conclusions in practical matters, their egotistical engrossment in their own subjects, are extreme examples of the bad effects of severing studies completely from their ordinary connections in life.

Overdoing the mechanical and automatic

"Drill"

(b) The danger in those studies where the main emphasis is upon acquisition of skill is just the reverse. The tendency is to take the shortest cuts possible to gain the required end. This makes the subjects mechanical, and thus restrictive of intellectual power. In the mastery of reading, writing, drawing, laboratory technique, etc., the need of economy of time and material, of neatness and accuracy, of promptness and uniformity, is so great that these things tend to become ends in themselves, irrespective of their influence upon general mental attitude. Sheer imitation, dictation of steps to be taken, mechanical drill, may give results most quickly and yet strengthen traits likely to be fatal to reflective power. The pupil is enjoined to do this and that specific thing, with no knowledge of any reason except that by so doing he gets his result most speedily; his mistakes are pointed out and corrected for him; he is kept at pure repetition of certain acts till they become automatic. Later, teachers wonder why the pupil reads with so little expression, and figures with so little intelligent consideration of the terms of his problem. In some educational dogmas and practices, the very idea of training mind seems to be hopelessly confused with that of a drill which hardly touches mind at all—or touches it for the worse—since it is wholly taken up with training skill in external execution. This method reduces the "training" of human beings to the level of animal training. Practical skill, modes of effective technique, can be intelligently, non-mechanically used, only when intelligence has played a part in their acquisition.

Wisdom versus information

(c) Much the same sort of thing is to be said regarding studies where emphasis traditionally falls upon bulk and accuracy of information. The distinction between information and wisdom is old, and yet requires constantly to be redrawn. Information is knowledge which is merely acquired and stored up; wisdom is knowledge operating in the direction of powers to the better living of life. Information, merely as information, implies no special training of intellectual capacity; wisdom is the finest fruit of that training. In school, amassing information always tends to escape from the ideal of wisdom or good judgment. The aim often seems to be—especially in such a subject as geography—to make the pupil what has been called a "cyclopedia of useless information." "Covering the ground" is the primary necessity; the nurture of mind a bad second. Thinking cannot, of course, go on in a vacuum; suggestions and inferences can occur only upon a basis of information as to matters of fact.

But there is all the difference in the world whether the acquisition of information is treated as an end in itself, or is made an integral portion of the training of thought. The assumption that information which has been accumulated apart from use in the recognition and solution of a problem may later on be freely employed at will by thought is quite false. The skill at the ready command of intelligence is the skill acquired with the aid of intelligence; the only information which, otherwise than by accident, can be put to logical use is that acquired in the course of thinking. Because their knowledge has been achieved in connection with the needs of specific situations, men of little book-learning are often able to put to effective use every ounce of knowledge they possess; while men of vast erudition are often swamped by the mere bulk of their learning, because memory, rather than thinking, has been operative in obtaining it.

§4. The Influence of Current Aims and Ideals

It is, of course, impossible to separate this somewhat intangible condition from the points just dealt with; for automatic skill and quantity of information are educational ideals which pervade the whole school. We may distinguish, however, certain tendencies, such as that to judge education from the standpoint of external results, instead of from that of the development of personal attitudes and habits. The ideal of the product, as against that of the mental process by which the product is attained, shows itself in both instruction and moral discipline.

External results versus processes

(a) In instruction, the external standard manifests itself in the importance attached to the "correct answer." No one other thing, probably, works so fatally against focussing the attention of teachers upon the training of mind as the domination of their minds by the idea that the chief thing is to get pupils to recite their lessons correctly. As long as this end is uppermost (whether consciously or unconsciously), training of mind remains an incidental and secondary consideration. There is no great difficulty in understanding why this ideal has such vogue. The large number of pupils to be dealt with, and the tendency of parents and school authorities to demand speedy and tangible evidence of progress, conspire to give it currency. Knowledge of subject-matter—not of children—is alone exacted of teachers by this aim; and, moreover, knowledge of subject-matter only in portions definitely prescribed and laid out, and hence mastered with comparative ease. Education that takes as its standard the improvement of the intellectual attitude and method of students demands more serious preparatory training, for it exacts sympathetic and intelligent insight into the workings of individual minds, and a very wide and flexible command of subject-matter—so as to be able to select and apply just what is needed when it is needed. Finally, the securing of external results is an aim that lends itself naturally to the mechanics of school administration—to examinations, marks, gradings, promotions, and so on.

Reliance upon others

(b) With reference to behavior also, the external ideal has a great influence. Conformity of acts to precepts and rules is the easiest, because most mechanical, standard to employ. It is no part of our present task to tell just how far dogmatic instruction, or strict adherence to custom, convention, and the commands of a social superior, should extend in moral training; but since problems of conduct are the deepest and most common of all the problems of life, the ways in which they are met have an influence that radiates into every other mental attitude, even those far remote from any direct or conscious moral consideration. Indeed, the deepest plane of the mental attitude of every one is fixed by the way in which problems of behavior are treated. If the function of thought, of serious inquiry and reflection, is reduced to a minimum in dealing with them, it is not reasonable to expect habits of thought to exercise great influence in less important matters. On the other hand, habits of active inquiry and careful deliberation in the significant and vital problems of conduct afford the best guarantee that the general structure of mind will be reasonable.

Chapter Five

The Means and End of Mental Training: The Psychological and The Logical

§ 1. Introductory: The Meaning of Logical

Special topic of this chapter

In the preceding chapters we have considered (i) what thinking is; (ii) the importance of its special training; (iii) the natural tendencies that lend themselves to its training; and (iv) some of the special obstacles in the way of its training under school conditions. We come now to the relation of logic to the purpose of mental training.

Three senses of term logical

The practical is the important meaning of logical

In its broadest sense, any thinking that ends in a conclusion is logical—whether the conclusion reached be justified or fallacious; that is, the term logical covers both the logically good and the illogical or the logically bad. In its narrowest sense, the term logical refers only to what is demonstrated to follow necessarily from premises that are definite in meaning and that are either self-evidently true, or that have been previously proved to be true. Stringency of proof is here the equivalent of the logical. In this sense mathematics and formal logic (perhaps as a branch of mathematics) alone are strictly logical. Logical, however, is used in a third sense, which is at once more vital and more practical; to denote, namely, the systematic care, negative and positive, taken to safeguard reflection so that it may yield the best results under the given conditions. If only the word artificial were associated with the idea of art, or expert skill gained through voluntary apprenticeship (instead of suggesting the factitious and unreal), we might say that logical refers to artificial thought.

Care, thoroughness, and exactness the marks of the logical

In this sense, the word logical is synonymous with wide-awake, thorough, and careful reflection—thought in its best sense (ante, p. 5). Reflection is turning a topic over in various aspects and in various lights so that nothing significant about it shall be overlooked—almost as one might turn a stone over to see what its hidden side is like or what is covered by it. Thoughtfulness means, practically, the same thing as careful attention; to give our mind to a subject is to give heed to it, to take pains with it. In speaking of reflection, we naturally use the words weigh, ponder, deliberate—terms implying a certain delicate and scrupulous balancing of things against one another. Closely related names are scrutiny, examination, consideration, inspection—terms which imply close and careful vision. Again, to think is to relate things to one another definitely, to "put two and two together" as we say. Analogy with the accuracy and definiteness of mathematical combinations gives us such expressions as calculate, reckon, account for; and even reason itself—ratio. Caution, carefulness, thoroughness, definiteness, exactness, orderliness, methodic arrangement, are, then, the traits by which we mark off the logical from what is random and casual on one side, and from what is academic and formal on the other.

Whole object of intellectual education is formation of logical disposition

False opposition of the logical and psychological

No argument is needed to point out that the educator is concerned with the logical in its practical and vital sense. Argument is perhaps needed to show that the intellectual (as distinct from the moral) end of education is entirely and only the logical in this sense; namely,the formation of careful, alert, and thorough habits of thinking. The chief difficulty in the way of recognition of this principle is a false conception of the relation between the psychological tendencies of an individual and his logical achievements. If it be assumed—as it is so frequently—that these have, intrinsically, nothing to do with each other, then logical training is inevitably regarded as something foreign and extraneous, something to be ingrafted upon the individual from without, so that it is absurd to identify the object of education with the development of logical power.

Opposing the natural to the logical

The conception that the psychology of individuals has no intrinsic connections with logical methods and results is held, curiously enough, by two opposing schools of educational theory. To one school, the natural is primary and fundamental; and its tendency is to make little of distinctly intellectual nurture. Its mottoes are freedom, self-expression, individuality, spontaneity, play, interest, natural unfolding, and so on. In its emphasis upon individual attitude and activity, it sets slight store upon organized subject-matter, or the material of study, and conceives method to consist of various devices for stimulating and evoking, in their natural order of growth, the native potentialities of individuals.

Neglect of the innate logical resources

Identification of logical with subject-matter, exclusively

The other school estimates highly the value of the logical, but conceives the natural tendency of individuals to be averse, or at least indifferent, to logical achievement. It relies upon subject-matter—upon matter already defined and classified. Method, then, has to do with the devices by which these characteristics may be imported into a mind naturally reluctant and rebellious. Hence its mottoes are discipline, instruction, restraint, voluntary or conscious effort, the necessity of tasks, and so on. From this point of view studies, rather than attitudes and habits, embody the logical factor in education. The mind becomes logical only by learning to conform to an external subject-matter. To produce this conformity, the study should first be analyzed (by text-book or teacher) into its logical elements; then each of these elements should be defined; finally, all of the elements should be arranged in series or classes according to logical formulæ or general principles. Then the pupil learns the definitions one by one; and progressively adding one to another builds up the logical system, and thereby is himself gradually imbued, from without, with logical quality.

Illustration from geography

This description will gain meaning through an illustration. Suppose the subject is geography. The first thing is to give its definition, marking it off from every other subject. Then the various abstract terms upon which depends the scientific development of the science are stated and defined one by one—pole, equator, ecliptic, zone—from the simpler units to the more complex which are formed out of them; then the more concrete elements are taken in similar series: continent, island, coast, promontory, cape, isthmus, peninsula, ocean, lake, coast, gulf, bay, and so on. In acquiring this material, the mind is supposed not only to gain important information, but, by accommodating itself to ready-made logical definitions, generalizations, and classifications, gradually to acquire logical habits.

From drawing

This type of method has been applied to every subject taught in the schools—reading, writing, music, physics, grammar, arithmetic. Drawing for example, has been taught on the theory that since all pictorial representation is a matter of combining straight and curved lines, the simplest procedure is to have the pupil acquire the ability first to draw straight lines in various positions (horizontal, perpendicular, diagonals at various angles), then typical curves; and finally, to combine straight and curved lines in various permutations to construct actual pictures. This seemed to give the ideal "logical" method, beginning with analysis into elements, and then proceeding in regular order to more and more complex syntheses, each element being defined when used, and thereby clearly understood.

Formal method

Even when this method in its extreme form is not followed, few schools (especially of the middle or upper elementary grades) are free from an exaggerated attention to forms supposedly employed by the pupil if he gets his result logically. It is thought that there are certain steps arranged in a certain order, which express preëminently an understanding of the subject, and the pupil is made to "analyze" his procedure into these steps, i.e. to learn a certain routine formula of statement. While this method is usually at its height in grammar and arithmetic, it invades also history and even literature, which are then reduced, under plea of intellectual training, to "outlines," diagrams, and schemes of division and subdivision. In memorizing this simulated cut and dried copy of the logic of an adult, the child generally is induced to stultify his own subtle and vital logical movement. The adoption by teachers of this misconception of logical method has probably done more than anything else to bring pedagogy into disrepute; for to many persons "pedagogy" means precisely a set of mechanical, self-conscious devices for replacing by somecast-iron external scheme the personal mental movement of the individual.

Reaction toward lack of form and method

A reaction inevitably occurs from the poor results that accrue from these professedly "logical" methods. Lack of interest in study, habits of inattention and procrastination, positive aversion to intellectual application, dependence upon sheer memorizing and mechanical routine with only a modicum of understanding by the pupil of what he is about, show that the theory of logical definition, division, gradation, and system does not work out practically as it is theoretically supposed to work. The consequent disposition—as in every reaction—is to go to the opposite extreme. The "logical" is thought to be wholly artificial and extraneous; teacher and pupil alike are to turn their backs upon it, and to work toward the expression of existing aptitudes and tastes. Emphasis upon natural tendencies and powers as the only possible starting-point of development is indeed wholesome. But the reaction is false, and hence misleading, in what it ignores and denies: the presence of genuinely intellectual factors in existing powers and interests.

Logic of subject-matter is logic of adult or trained mind

What is conventionally termed logical (namely, the logical from the standpoint of subject-matter) represents in truth the logic of the trained adult mind. Ability to divide a subject, to define its elements, and to group them into classes according to general principles represents logical capacity at its best point reached after thorough training. The mind that habitually exhibits skill in divisions, definitions, generalizations, and systematic recapitulations no longer needs training in logical methods. But it is absurd to suppose that a mind which needs training because it cannot perform these operations can begin where the expert mind stops.

The logical from the standpoint of subject-matter represents the goal, the last term of training, not the point of departure.

The immature mind has its own logic

Hence, the psychological and the logical represent the two ends of the same movement

In truth, the mind at every stage of development has its own logic. The error of the notion that by appeal to spontaneous tendencies and by multiplication of materials we may completely dismiss logical considerations, lies in overlooking how large a part curiosity, inference, experimenting, and testing already play in the pupil's life. Therefore it underestimates the intellectual factor in the more spontaneous play and work of individuals—the factor that alone is truly educative. Any teacher who is alive to the modes of thought naturally operative in the experience of the normal child will have no difficulty in avoiding the identification of the logical with a ready-made organization of subject-matter, as well as the notion that the only way to escape this error is to pay no attention to logical considerations. Such a teacher will have no difficulty in seeing that the real problem of intellectual education is the transformation of natural powers into expert, tested powers: the transformation of more or less casual curiosity and sporadic suggestion into attitudes of alert, cautious, and thorough inquiry. He will see that the psychological and the logical, instead of being opposed to each other (or even independent of each other), are connected as the earlier and the later stages in one continuous process of normal growth. The natural or psychological activities, even when not consciously controlled by logical considerations, have their own intellectual function and integrity; conscious and deliberate skill in thinking, when it is achieved, makes habitual or second nature. The first is already logical in spirit; the last, in presenting an ingrained disposition and attitude, is then as psychological (as personal) as any caprice or chance impulse could be.

§ 2. Discipline and Freedom

True and false notions of discipline

Discipline of mind is thus, in truth, a result rather than a cause. Any mind is disciplined in a subject in which independent intellectual initiative and control have been achieved. Discipline represents original native endowment turned, through gradual exercise, into effective power. So far as a mind is disciplined, control of method in a given subject has been attained so that the mind is able to manage itself independently without external tutelage. The aim of education is precisely to develop intelligence of this independent and effective type—a disciplined mind. Discipline is positive and constructive.

Discipline as drill

Discipline, however, is frequently regarded as something negative—as a painfully disagreeable forcing of mind away from channels congenial to it into channels of constraint, a process grievous at the time but necessary as preparation for a more or less remote future. Discipline is then generally identified with drill; and drill is conceived after the mechanical analogy of driving, by unremitting blows, a foreign substance into a resistant material; or is imaged after the analogy of the mechanical routine by which raw recruits are trained to a soldierly bearing and habits that are naturally wholly foreign to their possessors. Training of this latter sort, whether it be called discipline or not, is not mental discipline. Its aim and result are not habits of thinking, but uniform external modes of action. By failing to ask what he means by discipline, many a teacher is misled into supposing that he is developing mental force and efficiency by methods which in fact restrict and deaden intellectual activity, and which tend to create mechanical routine, or mental passivity and servility.

As independent power or freedom

Freedom and external spontaneity

When discipline is conceived in intellectual terms (as the habitual power of effective mental attack), it is identified with freedom in its true sense. For freedom of mind means mental power capable of independent exercise, emancipated from the leading strings of others, not mere unhindered external operation. When spontaneity or naturalness is identified with more or less casual discharge of transitory impulses, the tendency of the educator is to supply a multitude of stimuli in order that spontaneous activity may be kept up. All sorts of interesting materials, equipments, tools, modes of activity, are provided in order that there may be no flagging of free self-expression. This method overlooks some of the essential conditions of the attainment of genuine freedom.

Some obstacle necessary for thought

(a) Direct immediate discharge or expression of an impulsive tendency is fatal to thinking. Only when the impulse is to some extent checked and thrown back upon itself does reflection ensue. It is, indeed, a stupid error to suppose that arbitrary tasks must be imposed from without in order to furnish the factor of perplexity and difficulty which is the necessary cue to thought. Every vital activity of any depth and range inevitably meets obstacles in the course of its effort to realize itself—a fact that renders the search for artificial or external problems quite superfluous. The difficulties that present themselves within the development of an experience are, however, to be cherished by the educator, not minimized, for they are the natural stimuli to reflective inquiry. Freedom does not consist in keeping up uninterrupted and unimpeded external activity, but is something achieved through conquering, by personal reflection, a way out of the difficulties that prevent an immediate overflow and a spontaneous success.

Intellectual factors are natural

(b) The method that emphasizes the psychological and natural, but yet fails to see what an important part of the natural tendencies is constituted at every period of growth by curiosity, inference, and the desire to test, cannot secure a natural development. In natural growth each successive stage of activity prepares unconsciously, but thoroughly, the conditions for the manifestation of the next stage—as in the cycle of a plant's growth. There is no ground for assuming that "thinking" is a special, isolated natural tendency that will bloom inevitably in due season simply because various sense and motor activities have been freely manifested before; or because observation, memory, imagination, and manual skill have been previously exercised without thought. Only when thinking is constantly employed in using the senses and muscles for the guidance and application of observations and movements, is the way prepared for subsequent higher types of thinking.

Genesis of thought contemporaneous with genesis of any human mental activity

At present, the notion is current that childhood is almost entirely unreflective—a period of mere sensory, motor, and memory development, while adolescence suddenly brings the manifestation of thought and reason.

Adolescence is not, however, a synonym for magic. Doubtless youth should bring with it an enlargement of the horizon of childhood, a susceptibility to larger concerns and issues, a more generous and a more general standpoint toward nature and social life. This development affords an opportunity for thinking of a more comprehensive and abstract type than has previously obtained. But thinking itself remains just what it has been all the time: a matter of following up and testing the conclusions suggested by the facts and events of life. Thinking begins as soon as the baby who has lost the ball that he is playing with begins to foresee the possibility of something not yet existing—its recovery; and begins to forecast steps toward the realization of this possibility, and, by experimentation, to guide his acts by his ideas and thereby also test the ideas. Only by making the most of the thought-factor, already active in the experiences of childhood, is there any promise or warrant for the emergence of superior reflective power at adolescence, or at any later period.

Fixation of bad mental habits

(c) In any case positive habits are being formed: if not habits of careful looking into things, then habits of hasty, heedless, impatient glancing over the surface; if not habits of consecutively following up the suggestions that occur, then habits of haphazard, grasshopper-like guessing; if not habits of suspending judgment till inferences have been tested by the examination of evidence, then habits of credulity alternating with flippant incredulity, belief or unbelief being based, in either case, upon whim, emotion, or accidental circumstances. The only way to achieve traits of carefulness, thoroughness, and continuity (traits that are, as we have seen, the elements of the "logical") is by exercising these traits from the beginning, and by seeing to it that conditions call for their exercise.

Genuine freedom is intellectual, not external

Genuine freedom, in short, is intellectual; it rests in the trained power of thought, in ability to "turn things over," to look at matters deliberately, to judge whether the amount and kind of evidence requisite for decision is at hand, and if not, to tell where and how to seek such evidence. If a man's actions are not guided by thoughtful conclusions, then they are guided by inconsiderate impulse, unbalanced appetite, caprice, or the circumstances of the moment. To cultivate unhindered, unreflective external activity is to foster enslavement, for it leaves the person at the mercy of appetite, sense, and circumstance.

PART TWO

Logical Considerations

Chapter Six

The Analysis of a Complete Act of Thought

Object of Part Two

After a brief consideration in the first chapter of the nature of reflective thinking, we turned, in the second, to the need for its training. Then we took up the resources, the difficulties, and the aim of its training. The purpose of this discussion was to set before the student the general problem of the training of mind. The purport of the second part, upon which we are now entering, is giving a fuller statement of the nature and normal growth of thinking, preparatory to considering in the concluding part the special problems that arise in connection with its education.

In this chapter we shall make an analysis of the process of thinking into its steps or elementary constituents, basing the analysis upon descriptions of a number of extremely simple, but genuine, cases of reflective experience.

A simple case of practical deliberation

1. "The other day when I was down town on 16th Street a clock caught my eye. I saw that the hands pointed to 12.20. This suggested that I had an engagement at 124th Street, at one o'clock. I reasoned that as it had taken me an hour to come down on a surface car, I should probably be twenty minutes late if I returned the same way. I might save twenty minutes by a subway express. But was there a station near? If not, I might lose more than twenty minutes in looking for one. Then I thought of the elevated, and I saw there was such a line within two blocks. But where was the station? If it were several blocks above or below the street I was on, I should lose time instead of gaining it. My mind went back to the subway express as quicker than the elevated; furthermore, I remembered that it went nearer than the elevated to the part of 124th Street I wished to reach, so that time would be saved at the end of the journey. I concluded in favor of the subway, and reached my destination by one o'clock."

A simple case of reflection upon an observation

2. "Projecting nearly horizontally from the upper deck of the ferryboat on which I daily cross the river, is a long white pole, bearing a gilded ball at its tip. It suggested a flagpole when I first saw it; its color, shape, and gilded ball agreed with this idea, and these reasons seemed to justify me in this belief. But soon difficulties presented themselves. The pole was nearly horizontal, an unusual position for a flagpole; in the next place, there was no pulley, ring, or cord by which to attach a flag; finally, there were elsewhere two vertical staffs from which flags were occasionally flown. It seemed probable that the pole was not there for flag-flying.

"I then tried to imagine all possible purposes of such a pole, and to consider for which of these it was best suited: (a) Possibly it was an ornament. But as all the ferryboats and even the tugboats carried like poles, this hypothesis was rejected. (b) Possibly it was the terminal of a wireless telegraph. But the same considerations made this improbable. Besides, the more natural place for such a terminal would be the highest part of the boat, on top of the pilot house. (c) Its purpose might be to point out the direction in which the boat is moving.

"In support of this conclusion, I discovered that the pole was lower than the pilot house, so that the steersman could easily see it. Moreover, the tip was enough higher than the base, so that, from the pilot's position, it must appear to project far out in front of the boat. Moreover, the pilot being near the front of the boat, he would need some such guide as to its direction. Tugboats would also need poles for such a purpose. This hypothesis was so much more probable than the others that I accepted it. I formed the conclusion that the pole was set up for the purpose of showing the pilot the direction in which the boat pointed, to enable him to steer correctly."

A simple case of reflection involving experiment

3. "In washing tumblers in hot soapsuds and placing them mouth downward on a plate, bubbles appeared on the outside of the mouth of the tumblers and then went inside. Why? The presence of bubbles suggests air, which I note must come from inside the tumbler. I see that the soapy water on the plate prevents escape of the air save as it may be caught in bubbles. But why should air leave the tumbler? There was no substance entering to force it out. It must have expanded. It expands by

increase of heat or by decrease of pressure, or by both. Could the air have become heated after the tumbler was taken from the hot suds? Clearly not the air that was already entangled in the water. If heated air was the cause, cold air must have entered in transferring the tumblers from the suds to the plate. I test to see if this supposition is true by taking several more tumblers out. Some I shake so as to make sure of entrapping cold air in them. Some I take out holding mouth downward in order to prevent cold air from entering. Bubbles appear on the outside of every one of the former and on none of the latter. I must be right in my inference. Air from the outside must have been expanded by the heat of the tumbler, which explains the appearance of the bubbles on the outside.

"But why do they then go inside? Cold contracts. The tumbler cooled and also the air inside it. Tension was removed, and hence bubbles appeared inside. To be sure of this, I test by placing a cup of ice on the tumbler while the bubbles are still forming outside. They soon reverse."

The three cases form a series

These three cases have been purposely selected so as to form a series from the more rudimentary to more complicated cases of reflection. The first illustrates the kind of thinking done by every one during the day's business, in which neither the data, nor the ways of dealing with them, take one outside the limits of everyday experience. The last furnishes a case in which neither problem nor mode of solution would have been likely to occur except to one with some prior scientific training. The second case forms a natural transition; its materials lie well within the bounds of everyday, unspecialized experience; but the problem, instead of being directly involved in the person's business, arises indirectly out of his activity, and accordingly appeals to a somewhat theoretic and impartial interest. We shall deal, in a later chapter, with the evolution of abstract thinking out of that which is relatively practical and direct; here we are concerned only with the common elements found in all the types.

Five distinct steps in reflection

Upon examination, each instance reveals, more or less clearly, five logically distinct steps: (i) a felt difficulty; (ii) its location and definition;

(iii) suggestion of possible solution; (iv) development by reasoning of the bearings of the suggestion; (v) further observation and experiment leading to its acceptance or rejection; that is, the conclusion of belief or disbelief.

1. The occurrence of a difficulty

(a) in the lack of adaptation of means to end

1. The first and second steps frequently fuse into one. The difficulty may be felt with sufficient definiteness as to set the mind at once speculating upon its probable solution, or an undefined uneasiness and shock may come first, leading only later to definite attempt to find out what is the matter. Whether the two steps are distinct or blended, there is the factor emphasized in our original account of reflection—viz. the perplexity or problem. In the first of the three cases cited, the difficulty resides in the conflict between conditions at hand and a desired and intended result, between an end and the means for reaching it. The purpose of keeping an engagement at a certain time, and the existing hour taken in connection with the location, are not congruous. The object of thinking is to introduce congruity between the two. The given conditions cannot themselves be altered; time will not go backward nor will the distance between 16th Street and 124th Street shorten itself. The problem is the discovery of intervening terms which when inserted between the remoter end and the given means will harmonize them with each other.

(b) in identifying the character of an object

In the second case, the difficulty experienced is the incompatibility of a suggested and (temporarily) accepted belief that the pole is a flagpole, with certain other facts. Suppose we symbolize the qualities that suggest flagpole by the letters a, b, c; those that oppose this suggestion by the letters p, q, r. There is, of course, nothing inconsistent in the qualities themselves; but in pulling the mind to different and incongruous conclusions they conflict—hence the problem. Here the object is the discovery of some object (O), of which a, b, c, and p, q, r, may all be appropriate traits—just as, in our first case, it is to discover a course of action which will combine existing conditions and a remoter result in a single whole. The method of solution is also the same: discovery of intermediate qualities (the position of the pilot house, of the pole, the need of an index to the boat's direction) symbolized by d, g, l, o, which bind together otherwise incompatible traits.

(c) in explaining an unexpected event

In the third case, an observer trained to the idea of natural laws or uniformities finds something odd or exceptional in the behavior of the bubbles. The problem is to reduce the apparent anomalies to instances of well-established laws. Here the method of solution is also to seek for intermediary terms which will connect, by regular linkage, the seemingly extraordinary movements of the bubbles with the conditions known to follow from processes supposed to be operative.

2. Definition of the difficulty

2. As already noted, the first two steps, the feeling of a discrepancy, or difficulty, and the acts of observation that serve to define the character of the difficulty may, in a given instance, telescope together. In cases of striking novelty or unusual perplexity, the difficulty, however, is likely to present itself at first as a shock, as emotional disturbance, as a more or less vague feeling of the unexpected, of something queer, strange, funny, or disconcerting. In such instances, there are necessary observations deliberately calculated to bring to light just what is the trouble, or to make clear the specific character of the problem. In large measure, the existence or non-existence of this step makes the difference between reflection proper, or safeguarded critical inference and uncontrolled thinking. Where sufficient pains to locate the difficulty are not taken, suggestions for its resolution must be more or less random. Imagine a doctor called in to prescribe for a patient. The patient tells him some things that are wrong; his experienced eye, at a glance, takes in other signs of a certain disease. But if he permits the suggestion of this special disease to take possession prematurely of his mind, to become an accepted conclusion, his scientific thinking is by that much cut short. A large part of his technique, as a skilled practitioner, is to prevent the acceptance of the first suggestions that arise; even, indeed, to postpone the occurrence of any very definite suggestion till the trouble—the nature of the problem—has been thoroughly explored. In the case of a physician this proceeding is known as diagnosis, but a similar inspection

is required in every novel and complicated situation to prevent rushing to a conclusion. The essence of critical thinking is suspended judgment; and the essence of this suspense is inquiry to determine the nature of the problem before proceeding to attempts at its solution. This, more than any other thing, transforms mere inference into tested inference, suggested conclusions into proof.

3. Occurrence of a suggested explanation or possible solution

3. The third factor is suggestion. The situation in which the perplexity occurs calls up something not present to the senses: the present location, the thought of subway or elevated train; the stick before the eyes, the idea of a flagpole, an ornament, an apparatus for wireless telegraphy; the soap bubbles, the law of expansion of bodies through heat and of their contraction through cold. (a) Suggestion is the very heart of inference; it involves going from what is present to something absent. Hence, it is more or less speculative, adventurous. Since inference goes beyond what is actually present, it involves a leap, a jump, the propriety of which cannot be absolutely warranted in advance, no matter what precautions be taken. Its control is indirect, on the one hand, involving the formation of habits of mind which are at once enterprising and cautious; and on the other hand, involving the selection and arrangement of the particular facts upon perception of which suggestion issues. (b) The suggested conclusion so far as it is not accepted but only tentatively entertained constitutes an idea. Synonyms for this are supposition, conjecture, guess, hypothesis, and (in elaborate cases) theory. Since suspended belief, or the postponement of a final conclusion pending further evidence, depends partly upon the presence of rival conjectures as to the best course to pursue or the probable explanation to favor, cultivation of a variety of alternative suggestions is an important factor in good thinking.

4. The rational elaboration of an idea

4. The process of developing the bearings—or, as they are more technically termed, the implications—of any idea with respect to any problem, is termed reasoning. As an idea is inferred from given facts, so reasoning sets out from an idea. The idea of elevated road is developed into the idea of difficulty of locating station, length of time occupied on the journey, distance of station at the other end from place to be

reached. In the second case, the implication of a flagpole is seen to be a vertical position; of a wireless apparatus, location on a high part of the ship and, moreover, absence from every casual tugboat; while the idea of index to direction in which the boat moves, when developed, is found to cover all the details of the case.

Reasoning has the same effect upon a suggested solution as more intimate and extensive observation has upon the original problem. Acceptance of the suggestion in its first form is prevented by looking into it more thoroughly. Conjectures that seem plausible at first sight are often found unfit or even absurd when their full consequences are traced out. Even when reasoning out the bearings of a supposition does not lead to rejection, it develops the idea into a form in which it is more apposite to the problem. Only when, for example, the conjecture that a pole was an index-pole had been thought out into its bearings could its particular applicability to the case in hand be judged. Suggestions at first seemingly remote and wild are frequently so transformed by being elaborated into what follows from them as to become apt and fruitful. The development of an idea through reasoning helps at least to supply the intervening or intermediate terms that link together into a consistent whole apparently discrepant extremes (ante, p. 72).

5. Corroboration of an idea and formation of a concluding belief

5. The concluding and conclusive step is some kind of experimental corroboration, or verification, of the conjectural idea. Reasoning shows that if the idea be adopted, certain consequences follow. So far the conclusion is hypothetical or conditional. If we look and find present all the conditions demanded by the theory, and if we find the characteristic traits called for by rival alternatives to be lacking, the tendency to believe, to accept, is almost irresistible. Sometimes direct observation furnishes corroboration, as in the case of the pole on the boat. In other cases, as in that of the bubbles, experiment is required; that is, conditions are deliberately arranged in accord with the requirements of an idea or hypothesis to see if the results theoretically indicated by the idea actually occur. If it is found that the experimental results agree with the theoretical, or rationally deduced, results, and if there is reason to believe that only the conditions in question would yield such results, the confirmation is so strong as to induce a conclusion—at least until contrary facts shall indicate the advisability of its revision.

Thinking comes between observations at the beginning and at the end

Observation exists at the beginning and again at the end of the process: at the beginning, to determine more definitely and precisely the nature of the difficulty to be dealt with; at the end, to test the value of some hypothetically entertained conclusion. Between those two termini of observation, we find the more distinctively mental aspects of the entire thought-cycle: (i) inference, the suggestion of an explanation or solution; and (ii) reasoning, the development of the bearings and implications of the suggestion. Reasoning requires some experimental observation to confirm it, while experiment can be economically and fruitfully conducted onlyon the basis of an idea that has been tentatively developed by reasoning.

The trained mind one that judges the extent of each step advisable in a given situation

The disciplined, or logically trained, mind—the aim of the educative process—is the mind able to judge how far each of these steps needs to be carried in any particular situation. No cast-iron rules can be laid down. Each case has to be dealt with as it arises, on the basis of its importance and of the context in which it occurs. To take too much pains in one case is as foolish—as illogical—as to take too little in another. At one extreme, almost any conclusion that insures prompt and unified action may be better than any long delayed conclusion; while at the other, decision may have to be postponed for a long period—perhaps for a lifetime. The trained mind is the one that best grasps the degree of observation, forming of ideas, reasoning, and experimental testing required in any special case, and that profits the most, in future thinking, by mistakes made in the past. What is important is that the mind should be sensitive to problems and skilled in methods of attack and solution.

Chapter Seven

Systematic Inference: Induction and Deduction

§ 1. The Double Movement of Reflection

Back and forth between facts and meanings

The characteristic outcome of thinking we saw to be the organization of facts and conditions which, just as they stand, are isolated, fragmentary, and discrepant, the organization being effected through the introduction of connecting links, or middle terms. The facts as they stand are the data, the raw material of reflection; their lack of coherence perplexes and stimulates to reflection. There follows the suggestion of some meaning which, if it can be substantiated, will give a whole in which various fragmentary and seemingly incompatible data find their proper place. The meaning suggested supplies a mental platform, an intellectual point of view, from which to note and define the data more carefully, to seek for additional observations, and to institute, experimentally, changed conditions.

Inductive and deductive

There is thus a double movement in all reflection: a movement from the given partial and confused data to a suggested comprehensive (or inclusive) entire situation; and back from this suggested whole—which as suggested is a meaning, an idea—to the particular facts, so as to connect these with one another and with additional facts to which the suggestion has directed attention. Roughly speaking, the first of these movements is inductive; the second deductive. A complete act of thought involves both—it involves, that is, a fruitful interaction of observed (or recollected) particular considerations and of inclusive and far-reaching (general) meanings.

Hurry versus caution

This double movement to and from a meaning may occur, however, in a casual, uncritical way, or in a cautious and regulated manner. To think means, in any case, to bridge a gap in experience, to bind together facts or deeds otherwise isolated. But we may make only a hurried jump from one consideration to another, allowing our aversion to mental disquietude to override the gaps; or, we may insist upon noting the road traveled in making connections. We may, in short, accept readily any suggestion that seems plausible; or we may hunt out additional factors, new difficulties, to see whether the suggested conclusion really ends the matter. The latter method involves definite formulation of the connecting links; the statement of a principle, or, in logical phrase, the use of a universal. If we thus formulate the whole situation, the original data are transformed into premises of reasoning; the final belief is a logical or rational conclusion, not a mere de facto termination.

Continuity of relationship the mark of the latter

The importance of connections binding isolated items into a coherent single whole is embodied in all the phrases that denote the relation of premises and conclusions to each other. (1) The premises are called grounds, foundations, bases, and are said to underlie, uphold, support the conclusion. (2) We "descend" from the premises to the conclusion, and "ascend" or "mount" in the opposite direction—as a river may be continuously traced from source to sea or vice versa. So the conclusion springs, flows, or is drawn from its premises. (3) The conclusion—as the word itself implies—closes, shuts in, locks up together the various factors stated in the premises. We say that the premises "contain" the conclusion, and that the conclusion "contains" the premises, thereby marking our sense of the inclusive and comprehensive unity in which the elements of reasoning are bound tightly together. Systematic inference, in short, means the recognition of definite relations of interdependence between considerations previously unorganized and disconnected, this recognition being brought about by the discovery and insertion of new facts and properties.

Scientific induction and deduction

This more systematic thinking is, however, like the cruder forms in its double movement, the movement toward the suggestion or hypothesis and the movement back to facts. The difference is in the greater conscious care with which each phase of the process is performed. The conditions under which suggestions are allowed to spring up and develop are regulated. Hasty acceptance of any idea that is plausible, that seems to solve the difficulty, is changed into a conditional acceptance pending further inquiry. The idea is accepted as a working hypothesis, as something to guide investigation and bring to light new facts, not as a final conclusion. When pains are taken to make each aspect of the movement as accurate as possible, the movement toward building up the idea is known as inductive discovery (induction, for short); the movement toward developing, applying, and testing, as deductive proof (deduction, for short).

Particular and universal

While induction moves from fragmentary details (or particulars) to a connected view of a situation (universal), deduction begins with the latter and works back again to particulars, connecting them and binding them together. The inductive movement is toward discovery of a binding principle; the deductive toward its testing—confirming, refuting, modifying it on the basis of its capacity to interpret isolated details into a unified experience. So far as we conduct each of these processes in the light of the other, we get valid discovery or verified critical thinking.

Illustration from everyday experience

A commonplace illustration may enforce the points of this formula. A man who has left his rooms in order finds them upon his return in a state of confusion, articles being scattered at random. Automatically, the notion comes to his mind that burglary would account for the disorder. He has not seen the burglars; their presence is not a fact of observation, but is a thought, an idea. Moreover, the man has no special burglars in mind; it is the relation, the meaning of burglary—something general—that comes to mind. The state of his room is perceived and is particular, definite—exactly as it is; burglars are inferred, and have a general status.

The state of the room is a fact, certain and speaking for itself; the presence of burglars is a possible meaning which may explain the facts.

Of induction

So far there is an inductive tendency, suggested by particular and present facts. In the same inductive way, it occurs to him that his children are mischievous, and that they may have thrown the things about. This rival hypothesis (or conditional principle of explanation) prevents him from dogmatically accepting the first suggestion. Judgment is held in suspense and a positive conclusion postponed.

Of deduction

Then deductive movement begins. Further observations, recollections, reasonings are conducted on the basis of a development of the ideas suggested: if burglars were responsible, such and such things would have happened; articles of value would be missing. Here the man is going from a general principle or relation to special features that accompany it, to particulars—not back, however, merely to the original particulars (which would be fruitless or take him in a circle), but to new details, the actual discovery or nondiscovery of which will test the principle. The man turns to a box of valuables; some things are gone; some, however, are still there. Perhaps he has himself removed the missing articles, but has forgotten it. His experiment is not a decisive test. He thinks of the silver in the sideboard—the children would not have taken that nor would he absent-mindedly have changed its place. He looks; all the solid ware is gone. The conception of burglars is confirmed; examination of windows and doors shows that they have been tampered with. Belief culminates; the original isolated facts have been woven into a coherent fabric. The idea first suggested (inductively) has been employed to reason out hypothetically certain additional particulars not yet experienced, that ought to be there, if the suggestion is correct. Then new acts of observation have shown that the particulars theoretically called for are present, and by this process the hypothesis is strengthened, corroborated. This moving back and forth between the observed facts and the conditional idea is kept up till a coherent experience of an object is substituted for the experience of conflicting details—or else the whole matter is given up as a bad job.

Science is the same operations carefully performed

Sciences exemplify similar attitudes and operations, but with a higher degree of elaboration of the instruments of caution, exactness and thoroughness. This greater elaboration brings about specialization, an accurate marking off of various types of problems from one another, and a corresponding segregation and classification of the materials of experience associated with each type of problem. We shall devote the remainder of this chapter to a consideration of the devices by which the discovery, the development, and the testing of meanings are scientifically carried on.

§ 2. Guidance of the Inductive Movement

Guidance is indirect

Control of the formation of suggestion is necessarily indirect, not direct; imperfect, not perfect. Just because all discovery, all apprehension involving thought of the new, goes from the known, the present, to the unknown and absent, no rules can be stated that will guarantee correct inference. Just what is suggested to a person in a given situation depends upon his native constitution (his originality, his genius), temperament, the prevalent direction of his interests, his early environment, the general tenor of his past experiences, his special training, the things that have recently occupied him continuously or vividly, and so on; to some extent even upon an accidental conjunction of present circumstances. These matters, so far as they lie in the past or in external conditions, clearly escape regulation. A suggestion simply does or does not occur; this or that suggestion just happens, occurs, springs up. If, however, prior experience and training have developed an attitude of patience in a condition of doubt, a capacity for suspended judgment, and a liking for inquiry, indirect control of the course of suggestions is possible. The individual may return upon, revise, restate, enlarge, and analyze the facts out of which suggestion springs. Inductive methods, in the technical sense, all have to do with regulating the conditions under which observation, memory, and the acceptance of the testimony of others (the operations supplying the raw data) proceed.

Method of indirect regulation

Given the facts A B C D on one side and certain individual habits on the other, suggestion occurs automatically. But if the facts A B C D are carefully looked into and thereby resolved into the facts A′ B′′ R S, a suggestion will automatically present itself different from that called up by the facts in their first form. To inventory the facts, to describe exactly and minutely their respective traits, to magnify artificially those that are obscure and feeble, to reduce artificially those that are so conspicuous and glaring as to be distracting—these are ways of modifying the facts that exercise suggestive force, and thereby indirectly guiding the formation of suggested inferences.

Illustration from diagnosis

Consider, for example, how a physician makes his diagnosis—his inductive interpretation. If he is scientifically trained, he suspends—postpones—reaching a conclusion in order that he may not be led by superficial occurrences into a snap judgment. Certain conspicuous phenomena may forcibly suggest typhoid, but he avoids a conclusion, or even any strong preference for this or that conclusion until he has greatly (i) enlarged the scope of his data, and (ii) rendered them more minute. He not only questions the patient as to his feelings and as to his acts prior to the disease, but by various manipulations with his hands (and with instruments made for the purpose) brings to light a large number of facts of which the patient is quite unaware. The state of temperature, respiration, and heart-action is accurately noted, and their fluctuations from time to time are exactly recorded. Until this examination has worked out toward a wider collection and in toward a minuter scrutiny of details, inference is deferred.

Summary: definition of scientific induction

Scientific induction means, in short, all the processes by which the observing and amassing of data are regulated with a view to facilitating the formation of explanatory conceptions and theories. These devices are all directed toward selecting the precise facts to which weight and significance shall attach in forming suggestions or ideas. Specifically, this selective determination involves devices of (1) elimination by analysis of what is likely to be misleading and irrelevant, (2) emphasis of the important by collection and comparison of cases, (3) deliberate construction of data by experimental variation.

Elimination of irrelevant meanings

(1) It is a common saying that one must learn to discriminate between observed facts and judgments based upon them. Taken literally, such advice cannot be carried out; in every observed thing there is—if the thing have any meaning at all—some consolidation of meaning with what is sensibly and physically present, such that, if this were entirely excluded, what is left would have no sense. A says: "I saw my brother." The term brother, however, involves a relation that cannot be sensibly or physically observed; it is inferential in status. If A contents himself with saying, "I saw a man," the factor of classification, of intellectual reference, is less complex, but still exists. If, as a last resort, A were to say, "Anyway, I saw a colored object," some relationship, though more rudimentary and undefined, still subsists. Theoretically, it is possible that no object was there, only an unusual mode of nerve stimulation. None the less, the advice to discriminate what is observed from what is inferred is sound practical advice. Its working import is that one should eliminate or exclude those inferences as to which experience has shown that there is greatest liability to error. This, of course, is a relative matter. Under ordinary circumstances no reasonable doubt would attach to the observation, "I see my brother"; it would be pedantic and silly to resolve this recognition back into a more elementary form. Under other circumstances it might be a perfectly genuine question as to whether A saw even a colored thing, or whether the color was due to a stimulation of the sensory optical apparatus (like "seeing stars" upon a blow) or to a disordered circulation. In general, the scientific man is one who knows that he is likely to be hurried to a conclusion, and that part of this precipitancy is due to certain habits which tend to make him "read" certain meanings into the situation that confronts him, so that he must be on the lookout against errors arising from his interests, habits, and current preconceptions.

The technique of conclusion

The technique of scientific inquiry thus consists in various processes that tend to exclude over-hasty "reading in" of meanings; devices that aim to give a purely "objective" unbiased rendering of the data to be interpreted. Flushed cheeks usually mean heightened temperature; paleness means lowered temperature. The clinical thermometer records automatically the actual temperature and hence checks up the habitual associations that might lead to error in a given case. All the instrumentalities of observation—the various -meters and -graphs and -scopes—fill a part of their scientific rôle in helping to eliminate meanings supplied because of habit, prejudice, the strong momentary preoccupation of excitement and anticipation, and by the vogue of existing theories. Photographs, phonographs, kymographs, actinographs, seismographs, plethysmographs, and the like, moreover, give records that are permanent, so that they can be employed by different persons, and by the same person in different states of mind, i.e. under the influence of varying expectations and dominant beliefs. Thus purely personal prepossessions (due to habit, to desire, to after-effects of recent experience) may be largely eliminated. In ordinary language, the facts are objectively, rather than subjectively, determined. In this way tendencies to premature interpretation are held in check.

Collection of instances

(2) Another important method of control consists in the multiplication of cases or instances. If I doubt whether a certain handful gives a fair sample, or representative, for purposes of judging value, of a whole carload of grain, I take a number of handfuls from various parts of the car and compare them. If they agree in quality, well and good; if they disagree, we try to get enough samples so that when they are thoroughly mixed the result will be a fair basis for an evaluation. This illustration represents roughly the value of that aspect of scientific control in induction which insists upon multiplying observations instead of basing the conclusion upon one or a few cases.

This method not the whole of induction

So prominent, indeed, is this aspect of inductive method that it is frequently treated as the whole of induction. It is supposed that all inductive inference is based upon collecting and comparing a number of like cases. But in fact such comparison and collection is a secondary development within the process of securing a correct conclusion in some single case. If a man infers from a single sample of grain as to the grade of wheat of the car as a whole, it is induction and, under certain circumstances, a sound induction; other cases are resorted to simply for the sake of rendering that induction more guarded, and more probably correct. In like fashion, the reasoning that led up to the burglary idea in the instance already cited was inductive, though there was but one single case examined. The particulars upon which the general meaning (or relation) of burglary was grounded were simply the sum total of the unlike items and qualities that made up the one case examined. Had this case presented very great obscurities and difficulties, recourse might then have been had to examination of a number of similar cases. But this comparison would not make inductive a process which was not previously of that character; it would only render induction more wary and adequate. The object of bringing into consideration a multitude of cases is to facilitate the selection of the evidential or significant features upon which to base inference in some single case.

Contrast as important as likeness

Accordingly, points of unlikeness are as important as points of likeness among the cases examined. Comparison, without contrast, does not amount to anything logically. In the degree in which other cases observed or remembered merely duplicate the case in question, we are no better off for purposes of inference than if we had permitted our single original fact to dictate a conclusion. In the case of the various samples of grain, it is the fact that the samples are unlike, at least in the part of the carload from which they are taken, that is important. Were it not for this unlikeness, their likeness in quality would be of no avail in assisting inference. If we are endeavoring to get a child to regulate his conclusions about the germination of a seed by taking into account a number of instances, very little is gained if the conditions in all these instances closely approximate one another. But if one seed is placed in pure sand, another in loam, and another on blotting-paper, and if in each case there are two conditions, one with and another without moisture, the unlike factors tend to throw into relief the factors that are significant (or "essential") for reaching a conclusion. Unless, in short, the observer takes care to have the differences in the observed cases as extreme as conditions allow, and unless he notes unlikenesses as carefully as likenesses, he has no way of determining the evidential force of the data that confront him.

Importance of exceptions and contrary cases

Another way of bringing out this importance of unlikeness is the emphasis put by the scientist upon negative cases—upon instances which it would seem ought to fall into line but which as matter of fact do not. Anomalies, exceptions, things which agree in most respects but disagree in some crucial point, are so important that many of the devices of scientific technique are designed purely to detect, record, and impress upon memory contrasting cases. Darwin remarked that so easy is it to pass over cases that oppose a favorite generalization, that he had made it a habit not merely to hunt for contrary instances, but also to write down any exception he noted or thought of—as otherwise it was almost sure to be forgotten.

§ 3. Experimental Variation of Conditions

Experiment the typical method of introducing contrast factors

We have already trenched upon this factor of inductive method, the one that is the most important of all wherever it is feasible. Theoretically, one sample case of the right kind will be as good a basis for an inference as a thousand cases; but cases of the "right kind" rarely turn up spontaneously. We have to search for them, and we may have to make them. If we take cases just as we find them—whether one case or many cases—they contain much that is irrelevant to the problem in hand, while much that is relevant is obscure, hidden. The object of experimentation is the construction, by regular steps taken on the basis of a plan thought out in advance, of a typical, crucial case, a case formed with express reference to throwing light on the difficulty in question. All inductive methods rest upon regulation of the conditions of observation and memory; experiment is simply the most adequate regulation possible of these conditions. We try to make the observation such that every factor entering into it, together with the mode and the amount of its operation, may be open to recognition. Such making of observations constitutes experiment.

Three advantages of experiment

Such observations have many and obvious advantages over observations—no matter how extensive—with respect to which we simply wait for an event to happen or an object to present itself. Experiment overcomes the defects due to (a) the rarity, (b) the subtlety and minuteness (or the violence), and (c) the rigid fixity of facts as we ordinarily experience them. The following quotations from Jevons's Elementary Lessons in Logic bring out all these points:

(i) "We might have to wait years or centuries to meet accidentally with facts which we can readily produce at any moment in a laboratory; and it is probable that most of the chemical substances now known, and many excessively useful products would never have been discovered at all by waiting till nature presented them spontaneously to our observation."

This quotation refers to the infrequency or rarity of certain facts of nature, even very important ones. The passage then goes on to speak of the minuteness of many phenomena which makes them escape ordinary experience:

(ii) "Electricity doubtless operates in every particle of matter, perhaps at every moment of time; and even the ancients could not but notice its action in the loadstone, in lightning, in the Aurora Borealis, or in a piece of rubbed amber. But in lightning electricity was too intense and dangerous; in the other cases it was too feeble to be properly understood. The science of electricity and magnetism could only advance by getting regular supplies of electricity from the common electric machine or the galvanic battery and by making powerful electromagnets. Most, if not all, the effects which electricity produces must go on in nature, but altogether too obscurely for observation."

Jevons then deals with the fact that, under ordinary conditions of experience, phenomena which can be understood only by seeing them under varying conditions are presented in a fixed and uniform way.

(iii) "Thus carbonic acid is only met in the form of a gas, proceeding from the combustion of carbon; but when exposed to extreme pressure and cold, it is condensed into a liquid, and may even be converted into a snowlike solid substance. Many other gases have in like manner been liquefied or solidified, and there is reason to believe that every substance is capable of taking all three forms of solid, liquid, and gas, if only the conditions of temperature and pressure can be sufficiently varied. Mere observation of nature would have led us, on the contrary, to suppose that nearly all substances were fixed in one condition only, and could not be converted from solid into liquid and from liquid into gas."

Many volumes would be required to describe in detail all the methods that investigators have developed in various subjects for analyzing and restating the facts of ordinary experience so that we may escape from capricious and routine suggestions, and may get the facts in such a form and in such a light (or context) that exact and far-reaching explanations may be suggested in place of vague and limited ones. But these various devices of inductive inquiry all have one goal in view: the indirect regulation of the function of suggestion, or formation of ideas; and, in the main, they will be found to reduce to some combination of the three types of selecting and arranging subject-matter just described.

§ 4. Guidance of the Deductive Movement

Value of deduction for guiding induction

Before dealing directly with this topic, we must note that systematic regulation of induction depends upon the possession of a body of general principles that may be applied deductively to the examination or construction of particular cases as they come up. If the physician does not know the general laws of the physiology of the human body, he has little way of telling what is either peculiarly significant or peculiarly exceptional in any particular case that he is called upon to treat. If he knows the laws of circulation, digestion, and respiration, he can deduce the conditions that should normally be found in a given case. These considerations give a base line from which the deviations and abnormalities of a particular case may be measured. In this way, the nature of the problem at hand is located and defined. Attention is not wasted upon features which though conspicuous have nothing to do with the case; it is concentrated upon just those traits which are out of the way and hence require explanation. A question well put is half answered; i.e. a difficulty clearly apprehended is likely to suggest its own solution—while a vague and miscellaneous perception of the problem leads to groping and fumbling. Deductive systems are necessary in order to put the question in a fruitful form.

"Reasoning a thing out"

The control of the origin and development of hypotheses by deduction does not cease, however, with locating the problem. Ideas as they first present themselves are inchoate and incomplete. Deduction is their elaboration into fullness and completeness of meaning. The phenomena which the physician isolates from the total mass of facts that exist in front of him suggest, we will say, typhoid fever. Now this conception of typhoid fever is one that is capable of development. If there is typhoid, wherever there is typhoid, there are certain results, certain characteristic symptoms. By going over mentally the full bearing of the concept of typhoid, the scientist is instructed as to further phenomena to be found. Its development gives him an instrument of inquiry, of observation and experimentation. He can go to work deliberately to see whether the case presents those features that it should have if the supposition is valid. The deduced results form a basis for comparison with observed results. Except where there is a system of principles capable of being elaborated by theoretical reasoning, the process of testing (or proof) of a hypothesis is incomplete and haphazard.

Such reasoning implies systematized knowledge,

These considerations indicate the method by which the deductive movement is guided. Deduction requires a system of allied ideas which may be translated into one another by regular or graded steps. The question is whether the facts that confront us can be identified as typhoid fever. To all appearances, there is a great gap between them and typhoid. But if we can, by some method of substitutions, go through a series of intermediary terms, the gap may, after all, be easily bridged. Typhoid may mean p which in turn means o, which means n which means m, which is very similar to the data selected as the key to the problem.

Or definition and classification

One of the chief objects of science is to provide for every typical branch of subject-matter a set of meanings and principles so closely interknit that any one implies some other according to definite conditions, which under certain other conditions implies another, and so on. In this way, various substitutions of equivalents are possible, and reasoning can trace out, without having recourse to specific observations, very remote consequences of any suggested principle. Definition, general formulæ, and classification are the devices by which the fixation and elaboration of a meaning into its detailed ramifications are carried on. They are not ends in themselves—as they are frequently regarded even in elementary education—but instrumentalities for facilitating the development of a conception into the form where its applicability to given facts may best be tested.

The final control of deduction

The final test of deduction lies in experimental observation. Elaboration by reasoning may make a suggested idea very rich and very plausible, but it will not settle the validity of that idea. Only if facts can be observed (by methods either of collection or of experimentation), that agree in detail and without exception with the deduced results, are we justified in accepting the deduction as giving a valid conclusion. Thinking, in short, must end as well as begin in the domain of concrete observations, if it is to be complete thinking. And the ultimate educative value of all deductive processes is measured by the degree to which they become working tools in the creation and development of new experiences.

§ 5. Some Educational Bearings of the Discussion

Educational counterparts of false logical theories

Isolation of "facts"

Some of the points of the foregoing logical analysis may be clinched by a consideration of their educational implications, especially with reference to certain practices that grow out of a false separation by which each is thought to be independent of the other and complete in itself. (i) In some school subjects, or at all events in some topics or in some lessons, the pupils are immersed in details; their minds are loaded with disconnected items (whether gleaned by observation and memory, or accepted on hearsay and authority). Induction is treated as beginning and ending with the amassing of facts, of particular isolated pieces of information. That these items are educative only as suggesting a view of some larger situation in which the particulars are included and thereby accounted for, is ignored. In object lessons in elementary education and in laboratory instruction in higher education, the subject is often so treated that the student fails to "see the forest on account of the trees." Things and their qualities are retailed and detailed, without reference to a more general character which they stand for and mean. Or, in the laboratory, the student becomes engrossed in the processes of manipulation—irrespective of the reason for their performance, without recognizing a typical problem for the solution of which they afford the appropriate method. Only deduction brings out and emphasizes consecutive relationships, and only when relationships are held in view does learning become more than a miscellaneous scrap-bag.

Failure to follow up by reasoning

(ii) Again, the mind is allowed to hurry on to a vague notion of the whole of which the fragmentary facts are portions, without any attempt to become conscious of how they are bound together as parts of this whole. The student feels that "in a general way," as we say, the facts of the history or geography lesson are related thus and so; but "in a general way" here stands only for "in a vague way," somehow or other, with no clear recognition of just how.

The pupil is encouraged to form, on the basis of the particular facts, a general notion, a conception of how they stand related; but no pains are taken to make the student follow up the notion, to elaborate it and see just what its bearings are upon the case in hand and upon similar cases. The inductive inference, the guess, is formed by the student; if it happens to be correct, it is at once accepted by the teacher; or if it is false, it is rejected. If any amplification of the idea occurs, it is quite likely carried through by the teacher, who thereby assumes the responsibility for its intellectual development. But a complete, an integral, act of thought requires that the person making the suggestion (the guess) be responsible also for reasoning out its bearings upon the problem in hand; that he develop the suggestion at least enough to indicate the ways in which it applies to and accounts for the specific data of the case. Too often when a recitation does not consist in simply testing the ability of the student to display some form of technical skill, or to repeat facts and principles accepted on the authority of text-book or lecturer, the teacher goes to the opposite extreme; and after calling out the spontaneous reflections of the pupils, their guesses or ideas about the matter, merely accepts or rejects them, assuming himself the responsibility for their elaboration. In this way, the function of suggestion and of interpretation is excited, but it is not directed and trained. Induction is stimulated but is not carried over into the reasoning phase necessary to complete it.

In other subjects and topics, the deductive phase is isolated, and is treated as if it were complete in itself. This false isolation may show itself in either (and both) of two points; namely, at the beginning or at the end of the resort to general intellectual procedure.

Isolation of deduction by commencing with it

(iii) Beginning with definitions, rules, general principles, classifications, and the like, is a common form of the first error. This method has been such a uniform object of attack on the part of all educational reformers that it is not necessary to dwell upon it further than to note that the mistake is, logically, due to the attempt to introduce deductive considerations without first making acquaintance with the particular facts that create a need for the generalizing rational devices. Unfortunately, the reformer sometimes carries his objection too far, or rather locates it in the wrong place. He is led into a tirade against all definition, all systematization, all use of general principles, instead of confining himself to pointing out their futility and their deadness when not properly motivated by familiarity with concrete experiences.

Isolation of deduction from direction of new observations

(iv) The isolation of deduction is seen, at the other end, wherever there is failure to clinch and test the results of the general reasoning processes by application to new concrete cases. The final point of the deductive devices lies in their use in assimilating and comprehending individual cases. No one understands a general principle fully—no matter how adequately he can demonstrate it, to say nothing of repeating it—till he can employ it in the mastery of new situations, which, if they are new, differ in manifestation from the cases used in reaching the generalization. Too often the text-book or teacher is contented with a series of somewhat perfunctory examples and illustrations, and the student is not forced to carry the principle that he has formulated over into further cases of his own experience. In so far, the principle is inert and dead.

Lack of provision for experimentation

(v) It is only a variation upon this same theme to say that every complete act of reflective inquiry makes provision for experimentation—for testing suggested and accepted principles by employing them for the active construction of new cases, in which new qualities emerge. Only slowly do our schools accommodate themselves to the general advance of scientific method. From the scientific side, it is demonstrated that effective and integral thinking is possible only where the experimental method in some form is used. Some recognition of this principle is evinced in higher institutions of learning, colleges and high schools. But in elementary education, it is still assumed, for the most part, that the pupil's natural range of observations, supplemented by what he accepts on hearsay, is adequate for intellectual growth. Of course it is not necessary that laboratories shall be introduced under that name, much less that elaborate apparatus be secured; but the entire scientific history of humanity demonstrates that the conditions for complete mental activity will not be obtained till adequate provision is made for the carrying on of activities that actually modify physical conditions, and that books, pictures, and even objects that are passively observed but not manipulated do not furnish the provision required.

Chapter Eight

Judgement: The Interpretation of Facts

§ 1. The Three Factors of Judging

Good judgment

A man of good judgment in a given set of affairs is a man in so far educated, trained, whatever may be his literacy. And if our schools turn out their pupils in that attitude of mind which is conducive to good judgment in any department of affairs in which the pupils are placed, they have done more than if they sent out their pupils merely possessed of vast stores of information, or high degrees of skill in specialized branches. To know what is good judgment we need first to know what judgment is.

Judgment and inference

That there is an intimate connection between judgment and inference is obvious enough. The aim of inference is to terminate itself in an adequate judgment of a situation, and the course of inference goes on through a series of partial and tentative judgments. What are these units, these terms of inference when we examine them on their own account? Their significant traits may be readily gathered from a consideration of the operations to which the word judgment was originally applied: namely, the authoritative decision of matters in legal controversy—the procedure of the judge on the bench. There are three such features: (1) a controversy, consisting of opposite claims regarding the same objective situation; (2) a process of defining and elaborating these claims and of sifting the facts adduced to support them; (3) a final decision, or sentence, closing the particular matter in dispute and also serving as a rule or principle for deciding future cases.

Uncertainty the antecedent of judgment

1. Unless there is something doubtful, the situation is read off at a glance; it is taken in on sight, i.e. there is merely apprehension, perception, recognition, not judgment. If the matter is wholly doubtful, if it is dark and obscure throughout, there is a blind mystery and again no judgment occurs. But if it suggests, however vaguely, different meanings, rival possible interpretations, there is some point at issue, some matter at stake. Doubt takes the form of dispute, controversy; different sides compete for a conclusion in their favor. Cases brought to trial before a judge illustrate neatly and unambiguously this strife of alternative interpretations; but any case of trying to clear up intellectually a doubtful situation exemplifies the same traits. A moving blur catches our eye in the distance; we ask ourselves: "What is it? Is it a cloud of whirling dust? a tree waving its branches? a man signaling to us?" Something in the total situation suggests each of these possible meanings. Only one of them can possibly be sound; perhaps none of them is appropriate; yet some meaning the thing in question surely has. Which of the alternative suggested meanings has the rightful claim? What does the perception really mean? How is it to be interpreted, estimated, appraised, placed? Every judgment proceeds from some such situation.

Judgment defines the issue

2. The hearing of the controversy, the trial, i.e. the weighing of alternative claims, divides into two branches, either of which, in a given case, may be more conspicuous than the other. In the consideration of a legal dispute, these two branches are sifting the evidence and selecting the rules that are applicable; they are "the facts" and "the law" of the case. In judgment they are (a) the determination of the data that are important in the given case (compare the inductive movement); and (b) the elaboration of the conceptions or meanings suggested by the crude data (compare the deductive movement). (a) What portions or aspects of the situation are significant in controlling the formation of the interpretation? (b) Just what is the full meaning and bearing of the conception that is used as a method of interpretation? These questions are strictly correlative; the answer to each depends upon the answer to the other. We may, however, for convenience, consider them separately.

(a) by selecting what facts are evidence

(a) In every actual occurrence, there are many details which are part of the total occurrence, but which nevertheless are not significant in relation to the point at issue. All parts of an experience are equally present, but they are very far from being of equal value as signs or as evidences. Nor is there any tag or label on any trait saying: "This is important," or "This is trivial." Nor is intensity, or vividness or conspicuousness, a safe measure of indicative and proving value. The glaring thing may be totally insignificant in this particular situation, and the key to the understanding of the whole matter may be modest or hidden. Features that are not significant are distracting; they proffer their claims to be regarded as clues and cues to interpretation, while traits that are significant do not appear on the surface at all. Hence, judgment is required even in reference to the situation or event that is present to the senses; elimination or rejection, selection, discovery, or bringing to light must take place. Till we have reached a final conclusion, rejection and selection must be tentative or conditional. We select the things that we hope or trust are cues to meaning. But if they do not suggest a situation that accepts and includes them, we reconstitute our data, the facts of the case; for we mean, intellectually, by the facts of the case those traits that are used as evidence in reaching a conclusion or forming a decision.

Expertness in selecting evidence

No hard and fast rules for this operation of selecting and rejecting, or fixing upon the facts, can be given. It all comes back, as we say, to the good judgment, the good sense, of the one judging. To be a good judge is to have a sense of the relative indicative or signifying values of the various features of the perplexing situation; to know what to let go as of no account; what to eliminate as irrelevant; what to retain as conducive to outcome; what to emphasize as a clue to the difficulty.This power in ordinary matters we call knack, tact, cleverness; in more important affairs, insight, discernment. In part it is instinctive or inborn; but it also represents the funded outcome of long familiarity with like operations in the past. Possession of this ability to seize what is evidential or significant and to let the rest go is the mark of the expert, the connoisseur, the judge, in any matter.

Intuitive judgments

Mill cites the following case, which is worth noting as an instance of the extreme delicacy and accuracy to which may be developed this power of sizing up the significant factors of a situation. "A Scotch manufacturer procured from England, at a high rate of wages, a working dyer, famous for producing very fine colors, with the view of teaching to his other workmen the same skill. The workman came; but his method of proportioning the ingredients, in which lay the secret of the effects he produced, was by taking them up in handfuls, while the common method was to weigh them. The manufacturer sought to make him turn his handling system into an equivalent weighing system, that the general principles of his peculiar mode of proceeding might be ascertained. This, however, the man found himself quite unable to do, and could therefore impart his own skill to nobody. He had, from individual cases of his own experience, established a connection in his mind between fine effects of color and tactual perceptions in handling his dyeing materials; and from these perceptions he could, in any particular case, infer the means to be employed and the effects which would be produced." Long brooding over conditions, intimate contact associated with keen interest, thorough absorption in a multiplicity of allied experiences, tend to bring about those judgments which we then call intuitive; but they are true judgments because they are based on intelligent selection and estimation, with the solution of a problem as the controlling standard. Possession of this capacity makes the difference between the artist and the intellectual bungler.

Such is judging ability, in its completest form, as to the data of the decision to be reached. But in any case there is a certain feeling along for the way to be followed; a constant tentative picking out of certain qualities to see what emphasis upon them would lead to; a willingness to hold final selection in suspense; and to reject the factors entirely or relegate them to a different position in the evidential scheme if other features yield more solvent suggestions. Alertness, flexibility, curiosity are the essentials; dogmatism, rigidity, prejudice, caprice, arising from routine, passion, and flippancy are fatal.

(b) To decide an issue, the appropriate principles must also be selected

(b) This selection of data is, of course, for the sake of controlling the development and elaboration of the suggested meaning in the light of which they are to be interpreted. An evolution of conceptions thus goes on simultaneously with the determination of the facts; one possible meaning after another is held before the mind, considered in relation to the data to which it is applied, is developed into its more detailed bearings upon the data, is dropped or tentatively accepted and used. We do not approach any problem with a wholly naïve or virgin mind; we approach it with certain acquired habitual modes of understanding, with a certain store of previously evolved meanings, or at least of experiences from which meanings may be educed. If the circumstances are such that a habitual response is called directly into play, there is an immediate grasp of meaning. If the habit is checked, and inhibited from easy application, a possible meaning for the facts in question presents itself. No hard and fast rules decide whether a meaning suggested is the right and proper meaning to follow up. The individual's own good (or bad) judgment is the guide. There is no label on any given idea or principle which says automatically, "Use me in this situation"—as the magic cakes of *Alice in Wonderland* were inscribed "Eat me." The thinker has to decide, to choose; and there is always a risk, so that the prudent thinker selects warily, subject, that is, to confirmation or frustration by later events. If one is not able to estimate wisely what is relevant to the interpretation of a given perplexing or doubtful issue, it avails little that arduous learning has built up a large stock of concepts. For learning is not wisdom; information does not guarantee good judgment. Memory may provide an antiseptic refrigerator in which to store a stock of meanings for future use, but judgment selects and adopts the one used in a given emergency—and without an emergency (some crisis, slight or great) there is no call for judgment. No conception, even if it is carefully and firmly established in the abstract, can at first safely be more than a candidate for the office of interpreter. Only greater success than that of its rivals in clarifying dark spots, untying hard knots, reconciling discrepancies, can elect it or prove it a valid idea for the given situation.

Judging terminates in a decision or statement

3. The judgment when formed is a decision; it closes (or concludes) the question at issue. This determination not only settles that particular case, but it helps fix a rule or method for deciding similar matters in the future; as the sentence of the judge on the bench both terminates

that dispute and also forms a precedent for future decisions. If the interpretation settled upon is not controverted by subsequent events, a presumption is built up in favor of similar interpretation in other cases where the features are not so obviously unlike as to make it inappropriate. In this way, principles of judging are gradually built up; a certain manner of interpretation gets weight, authority. In short, meanings get standardized, they become logical concepts.

§ 2. The Origin and Nature of Ideas

Ideas are conjectures employed in judging

This brings us to the question of ideas in relation to judgments. Something in an obscure situation suggests something else as its meaning. If this meaning is at once accepted, there is no reflective thinking, no genuine judging. Thought is cut short uncritically; dogmatic belief, with all its attending risks, takes place. But if the meaning suggested is held in suspense, pending examination and inquiry, there is true judgment. We stop and think, we de-fer conclusion in order to in-fer more thoroughly. In this process of being only conditionally accepted, only for examination, meanings become ideas. That is to say, an idea is a meaning that is tentatively entertained, formed, and used with reference to its fitness to decide a perplexing situation—a meaning used as a tool of judgment.

Or tools of interpretation

Let us recur to our instance of a blur in motion appearing at a distance. We wonder what the thing is, i.e. what the blur means. A man waving his arms, a friend beckoning to us, are suggested as possibilities. To accept at once either alternative is to arrest judgment. But if we treat what is suggested as only a suggestion, a supposition, a possibility, it becomes an idea, having the following traits: (a) As merely a suggestion, it is a conjecture, a guess, which in cases of greater dignity we call a hypothesis or a theory. That is to say, it is a possible but as yet doubtful mode of interpretation. (b) Even though doubtful, it has an office to perform; namely, that of directing inquiry and examination. If this blur means a friend beckoning, then careful observation should show certain other traits. If it is a man driving unruly cattle, certain other traits should be found. Let us look and see if these traits are found. Taken merely as a doubt, an idea would paralyze inquiry. Taken merely as a certainty, it would arrest inquiry. Taken as a doubtful possibility, it affords a standpoint, a platform, a method of inquiry.

Pseudo-ideas

Ideas are not then genuine ideas unless they are tools in a reflective examination which tends to solve a problem. Suppose it is a question of having the pupil grasp the idea of the sphericity of the earth. This is different from teaching him its sphericity as a fact. He may be shown (or reminded of) a ball or a globe, and be told that the earth is round like those things; he may then be made to repeat that statement day after day till the shape of the earth and the shape of the ball are welded together in his mind. But he has not thereby acquired any idea of the earth's sphericity; at most, he has had a certain image of a sphere and has finally managed to image the earth after the analogy of his ball image. To grasp sphericity as an idea, the pupil must first have realized certain perplexities or confusing features in observed facts and have had the idea of spherical shape suggested to him as a possible way of accounting for the phenomena in question. Only by use as a method of interpreting data so as to give them fuller meaning does sphericity become a genuine idea. There may be a vivid image and no idea; or there may be a fleeting, obscure image and yet an idea, if that image performs the function of instigating and directing the observation and relation of facts.

Ideas furnish the only alternative to "hit or miss" methods

Logical ideas are like keys which are shaping with reference to opening a lock. Pike, separated by a glass partition from the fish upon which they ordinarily prey, will—so it is said—butt their heads against the glass until it is literally beaten into them that they cannot get at their food. Animals learn (when they learn at all) by a "cut and try" method; by doing at random first one thing and another thing and then preserving the things that happen to succeed. Action directed consciously by ideas—by suggested meanings accepted for the sake of experimenting with them—is the sole alternative both to bull-headed stupidity and to learning bought from that dear teacher—chance experience.

They are methods of indirect attack

It is significant that many words for intelligence suggest the idea of circuitous, evasive activity—often with a sort of intimation of even moral obliquity. The bluff, hearty man goes straight (and stupidly, it is implied) at some work. The intelligent man is cunning, shrewd (crooked), wily, subtle, crafty, artful, designing—the idea of indirection is involved. An idea is a method of evading, circumventing, or surmounting through reflection obstacles that otherwise would have to be attacked by brute force. But ideas may lose their intellectual quality as they are habitually used. When a child was first learning to recognize, in some hesitating suspense, cats, dogs, houses, marbles, trees, shoes, and other objects, ideas—conscious and tentative meanings—intervened as methods of identification. Now, as a rule, the thing and the meaning are so completely fused that there is no judgment and no idea proper, but only automatic recognition. On the other hand, things that are, as a rule, directly apprehended and familiar become subjects of judgment when they present themselves in unusual contexts: as forms, distances, sizes, positions when we attempt to draw them; triangles, squares, and circles when they turn up, not in connection with familiar toys, implements, and utensils, but as problems in geometry.

§ 3. Analysis and Synthesis

Judging clears up things: analysis

Through judging confused data are cleared up, and seemingly incoherent and disconnected facts brought together. Things may have a peculiar feeling for us, they may make a certain indescribable impression upon us; the thing may feel round (that is, present a quality which we afterwards define as round), an act may seem rude (or what we afterwards classify as rude), and yet this quality may be lost, absorbed, blended in the total value of the situation. Only as we need to use just that aspect of the original situation as a tool of grasping something perplexing or obscure in another situation, do we abstract or detach the quality so that it becomes individualized. Only because we need to characterize the shape of some new object or the moral quality of some new act, does the element of roundness or rudeness in the old experience detach itself, and stand out as a distinctive feature. If the element thus selected clears up what is otherwise obscure in the new experience, if it settles what is uncertain, it thereby itself gains in positiveness and definiteness of meaning. This point will meet us again in the following chapter; here we shall speak of the matter only as it bears upon the questions of analysis and synthesis.

Mental analysis is not like physical division

Misapprehension of analysis in education

Even when it is definitely stated that intellectual and physical analyses are different sorts of operations, intellectual analysis is often treated after the analogy of physical; as if it were the breaking up of a whole into all its constituent parts in the mind instead of in space. As nobody can possibly tell what breaking a whole into its parts in the mind means, this conception leads to the further notion that logical analysis is a mere enumeration and listing of all conceivable qualities and relations. The influence upon education of this conception has been very great. Every subject in the curriculum has passed through—or still remains in—what may be called the phase of anatomical or morphological method: the stage in which understanding the subject is thought to consist of multiplying distinctions of quality, form, relation, and so on, and attaching some name to each distinguished element. In normal growth, specific properties are emphasized and so individualized only when they serve to clear up a present difficulty. Only as they are involved in judging some specific situation is there any motive or use for analyses, i.e. for emphasis upon some element or relation as peculiarly significant.

Effects of premature formulation

The same putting the cart before the horse, the product before the process, is found in that overconscious formulation of methods of procedure so current in elementary instruction. The method that is employed in discovery, in reflective inquiry, cannot possibly be identified with the method that emerges after the discovery is made. In the genuine operation of inference, the mind is in the attitude of search, of hunting, of projection, of trying this and that; when the conclusion is reached, the search is at an end. The Greeks used to discuss: "How is learning (or inquiry) possible? For either we know already what we are after, and then we do not learn or inquire; or we do not know, and then we cannot inquire, for we do not know what to look for." The dilemma is at least suggestive, for it points to the true alternative: the use in inquiry of doubt, of tentative suggestion, of experimentation. After we have reached the conclusion, a reconsideration of the steps of the process to see what is helpful, what is harmful, what is merely useless, will assist in dealing more promptly and efficaciously with analogous problems in the future. In this way, more or less explicit method is gradually built up.

Method comes before its formulation

It is, however, a common assumption that unless the pupil from the outset consciously recognizes and explicitly states the method logically implied in the result he is to reach, he will have no method, and his mind will work confusedly or anarchically; while if he accompanies his performance with conscious statement of some form of procedure (outline, topical analysis, list of headings and subheadings, uniform formula) his mind is safeguarded and strengthened. As a matter of fact, the development of an unconscious logical attitude and habit must come first. A conscious setting forth of the method logically adapted for reaching an end is possible only after the result has first been reached by more unconscious and tentative methods, while it is valuable only when a review of the method that achieved success in a given case will throw light upon a new, similar case. The ability to fasten upon and single out (abstract, analyze) those features of one experience which are logically best is hindered by premature insistence upon their explicit formulation. It is repeated use that gives a method definiteness; and given this definiteness, precipitation into formulated statement should follow naturally. But because teachers find that the things which they themselves best understand are marked off and defined in clear-cut ways, our schoolrooms are pervaded with the superstition that children are to begin with already crystallized formulæ of method.

Judgment reveals the bearing or significance of facts: synthesis

As analysis is conceived to be a sort of picking to pieces, so synthesis is thought to be a sort of physical piecing together; and so imagined, it also becomes a mystery. In fact, synthesis takes place wherever we grasp the bearing of facts on a conclusion, or of a principle on facts. As analysis is emphasis, so synthesis is placing; the one causes the emphasized fact or property to stand out as significant; the other gives what is selected its context, or its connection with what is signified. Every judgment is analytic in so far as it involves discernment, discrimination, marking off the trivial from the important, the irrelevant from what points to a conclusion; and it is synthetic in so far as it leaves the mind with an inclusive situation within which the selected facts are placed.

Analysis and synthesis are correlative

Educational methods that pride themselves on being exclusively analytic or exclusively synthetic are therefore (so far as they carry out their boasts) incompatible with normal operations of judgment. Discussions have taken place, for example, as to whether the teaching of geography should be analytic or synthetic. The synthetic method is supposed to begin with the partial, limited portion of the earth's surface already familiar to the pupil, and then gradually piece on adjacent regions (the county, the country, the continent, and so on) till an idea of the entire globe is reached, or of the solar system that includes the globe. The analytic method is supposed to begin with the physical whole, the solar system or globe, and to work down through its constituent portions till the immediate environment is reached. The underlying conceptions are of physical wholes and physical parts. As matter of fact, we cannot assume that the portion of the earth already familiar to the child is such a definite object, mentally, that he can at once begin with it; his knowledge of it is misty and vague as well as incomplete. Accordingly, mental progress will involve analysis of it—emphasis of the features that are significant, so that they will stand out clearly. Moreover, his own locality is not sharply marked off, neatly bounded, and measured. His experience of it is already an experience that involves sun, moon, and stars as parts of the scene he surveys; it involves a changing horizon line as he moves about; that is, even his more limited and local experience involves far-reaching factors that take his imagination clear beyond his own street and village. Connection, relationship with a larger whole, is already involved. But his recognition of these relations is inadequate, vague, incorrect. He needs to utilize the features of the local environment which are understood to help clarify and enlarge his conceptions of the larger geographical scene to which they belong. At the same time, not till he has grasped the larger scene will many of even the commonest features of his environment become intelligible. Analysis leads to synthesis; while synthesis perfects analysis. As the pupil grows in comprehension of the vast complicated earth in its setting in space, he also sees more definitely the meaning of the familiar local details. This intimate interaction between selective emphasis and interpretation of what is selected is found wherever reflection proceeds normally. Hence the folly of trying to set analysis and synthesis over against each other.

Chapter Nine

Meaning or Conceptions and Understanding

§ 1. The Place of Meanings in Mental Life

Meaning is central

As in our discussion of judgment we were making more explicit what is involved in inference, so in the discussion of meaning we are only recurring to the central function of all reflection. For one thing to mean, signify, betoken, indicate, or point to, another we saw at the outset to be the essential mark of thinking. To find out what facts, just as they stand, mean, is the object of all discovery; to find out what facts will carry out, substantiate, support a given meaning, is the object of all testing. When an inference reaches a satisfactory conclusion, we attain a goal of meaning. The act of judging involves both the growth and the application of meanings. In short, in this chapter we are not introducing a new topic; we are only coming to closer quarters with what hitherto has been constantly assumed. In the first section, we shall consider the equivalence of meaning and understanding, and the two types of understanding, direct and indirect.

I. MEANING AND UNDERSTANDING

To understand is to grasp meaning

If a person comes suddenly into your room and calls out "Paper," various alternatives are possible. If you do not understand the English language, there is simply a noise which may or may not act as a physical stimulus and irritant. But the noise is not an intellectual object; it does not have intellectual value. To say that you do not understand it and that it has no meaning are equivalents. If the cry is the usual accompaniment of the delivery of the morning paper, the sound will have meaning, intellectual content; you will understand it. Or if you are eagerly awaiting the receipt of some important document, you may assume that the cry means an announcement of its arrival. If (in the third place) you understand the English language, but no context suggests itself from your habits and expectations, the word has meaning, but not the whole event. You are then perplexed and incited to think out, to hunt for, some explanation of the apparently meaningless occurrence. If you find something that accounts for the performance, it gets meaning; you come to understand it. As intelligent beings, we presume the existence of meaning, and its absence is an anomaly. Hence, if it should turn out that the person merely meant to inform you that there was a scrap of paper on the sidewalk, or that paper existed somewhere in the universe, you would think him crazy or yourself the victim of a poor joke. To grasp a meaning, to understand, to identify a thing in a situation in which it is important, are thus equivalent terms; they express the nerves of our intellectual life. Without them there is (a) lack of intellectual content, or (b) intellectual confusion and perplexity, or else (c) intellectual perversion—nonsense, insanity.

Knowledge and meaning

All knowledge, all science, thus aims to grasp the meaning of objects and events, and this process always consists in taking them out of their apparent brute isolation as events, and finding them to be parts of some larger whole suggested by them, which, in turn, accounts for, explains, interprets them; i.e. renders them significant. Suppose that a stone with peculiar markings has been found. What do these scratches mean? So far as the object forces the raising of this question, it is not understood; while so far as the color and form that we see mean to us a stone, the object is understood. It is such peculiar combinations of the understood and the nonunderstood that provoke thought. If at the end of the inquiry, the markings are decided to mean glacial scratches, obscure and perplexing traits have been translated into meanings already understood: namely, the moving and grinding power of large bodies of ice and the friction thus induced of one rock upon another. Something already understood in one situation has been transferred and applied to what is strange and perplexing in another, and thereby the latter has become plain and familiar, i.e. understood. This summary illustration discloses that our power to think effectively depends upon possession of a capital fund of meanings which may be applied when desired.

II. DIRECT AND INDIRECT UNDERSTANDING

Direct and circuitous understanding

In the above illustrations two types of grasping of meaning are exemplified. When the English language is understood, the person grasps at once the meaning of "paper." He may not, however, see any meaning or sense in the performance as a whole. Similarly, the person identifies the object on sight as a stone; there is no secret, no mystery, no perplexity about that. But he does not understand the markings on it. They have some meaning, but what is it? In one case, owing to familiar acquaintance, the thing and its meaning, up to a certain point, are one. In the other, the thing and its meaning are, temporarily at least, sundered, and meaning has to be sought in order to understand the thing. In one case understanding is direct, prompt, immediate; in the other, it is roundabout and delayed.

Interaction of the two types

Most languages have two sets of words to express these two modes of understanding; one for the direct taking in or grasp of meaning, the other for its circuitous apprehension, thus: γνωναι and ειδεναι in Greek; *noscere* and *scire* in Latin; *kennen* and *wissen* in German; *connaître* and *savoir* in French; while in English to be acquainted with and to know of or about have been suggested as equivalents. Now our intellectual life consists of a peculiar interaction between these two types of understanding. All judgment, all reflective inference, presupposes some lack of understanding, a partial absence of meaning. We reflect in order that we may get hold of the full and adequate significance of what happens. Nevertheless, something must be already understood, the mind must be in possession of some meaning which it has mastered, or else thinking is impossible. We think in order to grasp meaning, but none the less every extension of knowledge makes us aware of blind and opaque spots, where with less knowledge all had seemed obvious and natural. A scientist brought into a new district will find many things that he does not understand, where the native savage or rustic will be wholly oblivious to any meanings beyond those directly apparent. Some Indians brought to a large city remained stolid at the sight of mechanical wonders of bridge, trolley, and telephone, but were held spellbound by the sight of workmen climbing poles to repair wires. Increase of the store of meanings makes us conscious of new problems, while only through translation of the new perplexities into what is already familiar and plain do we understand or solve these problems. This is the constant spiral movement of knowledge.

Intellectual progress a rhythm

Our progress in genuine knowledge always consists in part in the discovery of something not understood in what had previously been taken for granted as plain, obvious, matter-of-course, and in part in the use of meanings that are directly grasped without question, as instruments for getting hold of obscure, doubtful, and perplexing meanings. No object is so familiar, so obvious, so commonplace that it may not unexpectedly present, in a novel situation, some problem, and thus arouse reflection in order to understand it. No object or principle is so strange, peculiar, or remote that it may not be dwelt upon till its meaning becomes familiar—taken in on sight without reflection. We may come to see, perceive, recognize, grasp, seize, lay hold of principles, laws, abstract truths—i.e. to understand their meaning in very immediate fashion. Our intellectual progress consists, as has been said, in a rhythm of direct understanding—technically called apprehension—with indirect, mediated understanding—technically called comprehension.

§ 2. The Process of Acquiring Meanings

Familiarity

The first problem that comes up in connection with direct understanding is how a store of directly apprehensible meanings is built up. How do we learn to view things on sight as significant members of a situation, or as having, as a matter of course, specific meanings? Our chief difficulty in answering this question lies in the thoroughness with which the lesson of familiar things has been learnt. Thought can more easily traverse an unexplored region than it can undo what has been so thoroughly done as to be ingrained in unconscious habit. We apprehend chairs, tables, books, trees, horses, clouds, stars, rain, so promptly and directly that it is hard to realize that as meanings they had once to be acquired—the meanings are now so much parts of the things themselves.

Confusion is prior to familiarity

In an often quoted passage, Mr. James has said: "The baby, assailed by eyes, ears, nose, skin, and entrails at once, feels it all as one great blooming, buzzing confusion." Mr. James is speaking of a baby's world taken as a whole; the description, however, is equally applicable to the way any new thing strikes an adult, so far as the thing is really new and strange. To the traditional "cat in a strange garret," everything is blurred and confused; the wonted marks that label things so as to separate them from one another are lacking. Foreign languages that we do not understand always seem jabberings, babblings, in which it is impossible to fix a definite, clear-cut, individualized group of sounds. The countryman in the crowded city street, the landlubber at sea, the ignoramus in sport at a contest between experts in a complicated game, are further instances. Put an unexperienced man in a factory, and at first the work seems to him a meaningless medley. All strangers of another race proverbially look alike to the visiting foreigner. Only gross differences of size or color are perceived by an outsider in a flock of sheep, each of which is perfectly individualized to the shepherd. A diffusive blur and an indiscriminately shifting suction characterize what we do not understand. The problem of the acquisition of meaning by things, or (stated in another way) of forming habits of simple apprehension, is thus the problem of introducing (i) definiteness and distinction and (ii) consistency or stability of meaning into what is otherwise vague and wavering.

Practical responses clarify confusion

The acquisition of definiteness and of coherency (or constancy) of meanings is derived primarily from practical activities. By rolling an object, the child makes its roundness appreciable; by bouncing it, he singles out its elasticity; by throwing it, he makes weight its conspicuous distinctive factor. Not through the senses, but by means of the reaction, the responsive adjustment, is the impression made distinctive, and given a character marked off from other qualities that call out unlike reactions. Children, for example, are usually quite slow in apprehending differences of color. Differences from the standpoint of the adult so glaring that it is impossible not to note them are recognized and recalled with great difficulty. Doubtless they do not all feel alike, but there is no intellectual recognition of what makes the difference. The redness or greenness or blueness of the object does not tend to call out a reaction that is sufficiently peculiar to give prominence or distinction to the color trait. Gradually, however, certain characteristic habitual responses associate themselves with certain things; the white becomes the sign, say, of milk and sugar, to which the child reacts favorably; blue becomes the sign of a dress that the child likes to wear, and so on: and the distinctive reactions tend to single out color qualities from other things in which they had been submerged.

We identify by use or function

Take another example. We have little difficulty in distinguishing from one another rakes, hoes, plows and harrows, shovels and spades. Each has its own associated characteristic use and function. We may have, however, great difficulty in recalling the difference between serrate and dentate, ovoid and obovoid, in the shapes and edges of leaves, or between acids in ic and in ous. There is some difference; but just what? Or, we know what the difference is; but which is which? Variations in form, size, color, and arrangement of parts have much less to do, and the uses, purposes, and functions of things and of their parts much more to do, with distinctness of character and meaning than we should be likely to think. What misleads us is the fact that the qualities of form, size, color, and so on, are now so distinct that we fail to see that the problem is precisely to account for the way in which they originally obtained their definiteness and conspicuousness. So far as we sit passive before objects, they are not distinguished out of a vague blur which swallows them all. Differences in the pitch and intensity of sounds leave behind a different feeling, but until we assume different attitudes toward them, or do something special in reference to them, their vague difference cannot be intellectually gripped and retained.

Children's drawings illustrate domination by value

Children's drawings afford a further exemplification of the same principle. Perspective does not exist, for the child's interest is not in pictorial representation, but in the things represented; and while perspective is essential to the former, it is no part of the characteristic uses and values of the things themselves. The house is drawn with transparent walls, because the rooms, chairs, beds, people inside, are the important things in the house-meaning; smoke always comes out of the chimney—otherwise, why have a chimney at all? At Christmas time, the stockings may be drawn almost as large as the house or even so large that they have to be put outside of it:—in any case, it is the scale of values in use that furnishes the scale for their qualities, the pictures being diagrammatic reminders of these values, not impartial records of physical and sensory qualities. One of the chief difficulties felt by most persons in learning the art of pictorial representation is that habitual uses and results of use have become so intimately read into the character of things that it is practically impossible to shut them out at will.

As do sounds used as language signs

The acquiring of meaning by sounds, in virtue of which they become words, is perhaps the most striking illustration that can be found of the way in which mere sensory stimuli acquire definiteness and constancy of meaning and are thereby themselves defined and interconnected for purposes of recognition. Language is a specially good example because there are hundreds or even thousands of words in which meaning is now so thoroughly consolidated with physical qualities as to be directly apprehended, while in the case of words it is easier to recognize that this connection has been gradually and laboriously acquired than in the case of physical objects such as chairs, tables, buttons, trees, stones, hills, flowers, and so on, where it seems as if the union of intellectual character and meaning with the physical fact were aboriginal, and thrust upon us passively rather than acquired through active explorations. And in the case of the meaning of words, we see readily that it is by making sounds and noting the results which follow, by listening to the sounds of others and watching the activities which accompany them, that a given sound finally becomes the stable bearer of a meaning.

Summary

Familiar acquaintance with meanings thus signifies that we have acquired in the presence of objects definite attitudes of response which lead us, without reflection, to anticipate certain possible consequences. The definiteness of the expectation defines the meaning or takes it out of the vague and pulpy; its habitual, recurrent character gives the meaning constancy, stability, consistency, or takes it out of the fluctuating and wavering.

§ 3. Conceptions and Meaning

A conception is a definite meaning

The word meaning is a familiar everyday term; the words conception, notion, are both popular and technical terms. Strictly speaking, they involve, however, nothing new; any meaning sufficiently individualized to be directly grasped and readily used, and thus fixed by a word, is a conception or notion. Linguistically, every common noun is the carrier of a meaning, while proper nouns and common nouns with the word this or that prefixed, refer to the things in which the meanings are exemplified. That thinking both employs and expands notions, conceptions, is then simply saying that in inference and judgment we use meanings, and that this use also corrects and widens them.

Which is standardized

Various persons talk about an object not physically present, and yet all get the same material of belief. The same person in different moments often refers to the same object or kind of objects. The sense experience, the physical conditions, the psychological conditions, vary, but the same meaning is conserved. If pounds arbitrarily changed their weight, and foot rules their length, while we were using them, obviously we could not weigh nor measure. This would be our intellectual position if meanings could not be maintained with a certain stability and constancy through a variety of physical and personal changes.

By it we identify the unknown and supplement the sensibly present and also systematize things

To insist upon the fundamental importance of conceptions would, accordingly, only repeat what has been said. We shall merely summarize, saying that conceptions, or standard meanings, are instruments (i) of identification, (ii) of supplementation, and (iii) of placing in a system. Suppose a little speck of light hitherto unseen is detected in the heavens. Unless there is a store of meanings to fall back upon as tools of inquiry and reasoning, that speck of light will remain just what it is to the senses—a mere speck of light. For all that it leads to, it might as well be a mere irritation of the optic nerve. Given the stock of meanings acquired in prior experience, this speck of light is mentally attacked by means of appropriate concepts. Does it indicate asteroid, or comet, or a new-forming sun, or a nebula resulting from some cosmic collision or disintegration? Each of these conceptions has its own specific and differentiating characters, which are then sought for by minute and persistent inquiry. As a result, then, the speck is identified, we will say, as a comet. Through a standard meaning, it gets identity and stability of character. Supplementation then takes place. All the known qualities of comets are read into this particular thing, even though they have not been as yet observed. All that the astronomers of the past have learned about the paths and structure of comets becomes available capital with which to interpret the speck of light. Finally, this comet-meaning is itself not isolated; it is a related portion of the whole system of astronomic knowledge. Suns, planets, satellites, nebulæ, comets, meteors, star dust—all these conceptions have a certain mutuality of reference and interaction, and when the speck of light is identified as meaning a comet, it is at once adopted as a full member in this vast kingdom of beliefs.

Importance of system to knowledge

Darwin, in an autobiographical sketch, says that when a youth he told the geologist, Sidgwick, of finding a tropical shell in a certain gravel pit. Thereupon Sidgwick said it must have been thrown there by some person, adding: "But if it were really embedded there, it would be the greatest misfortune to geology, because it would overthrow all that we know about the superficial deposits of the Midland Counties"—since they were glacial. And then Darwin adds: "I was then utterly astonished at Sidgwick not being delighted at so wonderful a fact as a tropical shell being found near the surface in the middle of England. Nothing before had made me thoroughly realize that science consists in grouping facts so that general laws or conclusions may be drawn from them." This instance (which might, of course, be duplicated from any branch of science) indicates how scientific notions make explicit the systematizing tendency involved in all use of concepts.

§ 4. What Conceptions are Not

The idea that a conception is a meaning that supplies a standard rule for the identification and placing of particulars may be contrasted with some current misapprehensions of its nature.

A concept is not a bare residue

1. Conceptions are not derived from a multitude of different definite objects by leaving out the qualities in which they differ and retaining those in which they agree. The origin of concepts is sometimes described to be as if a child began with a lot of different particular things, say particular dogs; his own Fido, his neighbor's Carlo, his cousin's Tray. Having all these different objects before him, he analyzes them into a lot of different qualities, say (a) color, (b) size, (c) shape, (d) number of legs, (e) quantity and quality of hair, (f) digestive organs, and so on; and then strikes out all the unlike qualities (such as color, size, shape, hair), retaining traits such as quadruped and domesticated, which they all have in general.

But an active attitude

As a matter of fact, the child begins with whatever significance he has got out of the one dog he has seen, heard, and handled. He has found that he can carry over from one experience of this object to subsequent experience certain expectations of certain characteristic modes of behavior—may expect these even before they show themselves. He tends to assume this attitude of anticipation whenever any clue or stimulus presents itself; whenever the object gives him any excuse for it. Thus he might call cats little dogs, or horses big dogs. But finding that other expected traits and modes of behavior are not fulfilled, he is forced to throw out certain traits from the dog-meaning, while by contrast certain other traits are selected and emphasized. As he further applies the meaning to other dogs, the dog-meaning gets still further defined and refined. He does not begin with a lot of ready-made objects from which he extracts a common meaning; he tries to apply to every new experience whatever from his old experience will help him understand it, and as this process of constant assumption and experimentation is fulfilled and refuted by results, his conceptions get body and clearness.

It is general because of its application

2. Similarly, conceptions are general because of their use and application, not because of their ingredients. The view of the origin of conception in an impossible sort of analysis has as its counterpart the idea that the conception is made up out of all the like elements that remain after dissection of a number of individuals. Not so; the moment a meaning is gained, it is a working tool of further apprehensions, an instrument of understanding other things. Thereby the meaning is extended to cover them. Generality resides in application to the comprehension of new cases, not in constituent parts. A collection of traits left as the common residuum, the caput mortuum, of a million objects, would be merely a collection, an inventory or aggregate, not a general idea; a striking trait emphasized in any one experience which then served to help understand some one other experience, would become, in virtue of that service of application, in so far general. Synthesis is not a matter of mechanical addition, but of application of something discovered in one case to bring other cases into line.

§ 5. Definition and Organization of Meanings

Definiteness versus vagueness: In the abstract meaning is intension, In its application it is extension

A being that cannot understand at all is at least protected from misunderstandings. But beings that get knowledge by means of inferring and interpreting, by judging what things signify in relation to one another, are constantly exposed to the danger of mis-apprehension, mis-understanding, mis-taking—taking a thing amiss. A constant source of misunderstanding and mistake is indefiniteness of meaning. Through vagueness of meaning we misunderstand other people, things, and ourselves; through its ambiguity we distort and pervert. Conscious distortion of meaning may be enjoyed as nonsense; erroneous meanings, if clear-cut, may be followed up and got rid of. But vague meanings are too gelatinous to offer matter for analysis, and too pulpy to afford support to other beliefs. They evade testing and responsibility. Vagueness disguises the unconscious mixing together of different meanings, and facilitates the substitution of one meaning for another, and covers up the failure to have any precise meaning at all. It is the aboriginal logical sin—the source from which flow most bad intellectual consequences.

Totally to eliminate indefiniteness is impossible; to reduce it in extent and in force requires sincerity and vigor. To be clear or perspicuous a meaning must be detached, single, self-contained, homogeneous as it were, throughout. The technical name for any meaning which is thus individualized is intension. The process of arriving at such units of meaning (and of stating them when reached) is definition. The intension of the terms man, river, seed, honesty, capital, supreme court, is the meaning that exclusively and characteristically attaches to those terms. This meaning is set forth in the definitions of those words. The test of the distinctness of a meaning is that it shall successfully mark off a group of things that exemplify the meaning from other groups, especially of those objects that convey nearly allied meanings. The river-meaning (or character) must serve to designate the Rhone, the Rhine, the Mississippi, the Hudson, the Wabash, in spite of their varieties of place, length, quality of water; and must be such as not to suggest ocean currents, ponds, or brooks. This use of a meaning to mark off and group together a variety of distinct existences constitutes its extension.

Definition and division

As definition sets forth intension, so division (or the reverse process, classification) expounds extension. Intension and extension, definition and division, are clearly correlative; in language previously used, intension is meaning as a principle of identifying particulars; extension is the group of particulars identified and distinguished. Meaning, as extension, would be wholly in the air or unreal, did it not point to some object or group of objects; while objects would be as isolated and independent intellectually as they seem to be spatially, were they not bound into groups or classes on the basis of characteristic meanings which they constantly suggest and exemplify. Taken together, definition and division put us in possession of individualized or definite meanings and indicate to what group of objects meanings refer. They typify the fixation and the organization of meanings. In the degree in which the meanings of any set of experiences are so cleared up as to serve as principles for grouping those experiences in relation to one another, that set of particulars becomes a science; i.e. definition and classification are the marks of a science, as distinct from both unrelated heaps of miscellaneous information and from the habits that introduce coherence into our experience without our being aware of their operation.

Definitions are of three types, denotative, expository, scientific. Of these, the first and third are logically important, while the expository type is socially and pedagogically important as an intervening step.

We define by picking out

I. Denotative. A blind man can never have an adequate understanding of the meaning of color and red; a seeing person can acquire the knowledge only by having certain things designated in such a way as to fix attention upon some of their qualities. This method of delimiting a meaning by calling out a certain attitude toward objects may be called denotative or indicative. It is required for all sense qualities—sounds, tastes, colors—and equally for all emotional and moral qualities. The meanings of honesty, sympathy, hatred, fear, must be grasped by having them presented in an individual's first-hand experience. The reaction of educational reformers against linguistic and bookish training has always taken the form of demanding recourse to personal experience. However advanced the person is in knowledge and in scientific training, understanding of a new subject, or a new aspect of an old subject, must always be through these acts of experiencing directly the existence or quality in question.

And also by combining what is already more definite,

2. Expository. Given a certain store of meanings which have been directly or denotatively marked out, language becomes a resource by which imaginative combinations and variations may be built up. A color may be defined to one who has not experienced it as lying between green and blue; a tiger may be defined (i.e. the idea of it made more definite) by selecting some qualities from known members of the cat tribe and combining them with qualities of size and weight derived from other objects. Illustrations are of the nature of expository definitions; so are the accounts of meanings given in a dictionary. By taking better-known meanings and associating them,—the attained store of meanings of the community in which one resides is put at one's disposal. But in themselves these definitions are secondhand and conventional; there is danger that instead of inciting one to effort after personal experiences that will exemplify and verify them, they will be accepted on authority as substitutes.

And by discovering method of production

3. Scientific. Even popular definitions serve as rules for identifying and classifying individuals, but the purpose of such identifications and classifications is mainly practical and social, not intellectual. To conceive the whale as a fish does not interfere with the success of whalers, nor does it prevent recognition of a whale when seen, while to conceive it not as fish but as mammal serves the practical end equally well, and also furnishes a much more valuable principle for scientific identification and classification. Popular definitions select certain fairly obvious traits as keys to classification. Scientific definitions select conditions of causation, production, and generation as their characteristic material. The traits used by the popular definition do not help us to understand why an object has its common meanings and qualities; they simply state the fact that it does have them. Causal and genetic definitions fix upon the way an object is constructed as the key to its being a certain kind of object, and thereby explain why it has its class or common traits.

Contrast of causal and descriptive definitions: Science is the most perfect type of knowledge because it uses causal definitions

If, for example, a layman of considerable practical experience were asked what he meant or understood by metal, he would probably reply in terms of the qualities useful (i) in recognizing any given metal and (ii) in the arts. Smoothness, hardness, glossiness, and brilliancy, heavy weight for its size, would probably be included in his definition, because such traits enable us to identify specific things when we see and touch them; the serviceable properties of capacity for being hammered and pulled without breaking, of being softened by heat and hardened by cold, of retaining the shape and form given, of resistance to pressure and decay, would probably be included—whether or not such terms as malleable or fusible were used. Now a scientific conception, instead of using, even with additions, traits of this kind, determines meaning on a different basis. The present definition of metal is about like this: Metal means any chemical element that enters into combination with oxygen so as to form a base, i.e. a compound that combines with an acid to form a salt. This scientific definition is founded, not on directly perceived qualities nor on directly useful properties, but on the way in which certain things are causally related to other things; i.e. it denotes a relation. As chemical concepts become more and more those of relationships of interaction in constituting other substances, so physical concepts express more and more relations of operation: mathematical, as expressing functions of dependence and order of grouping; biological, relations of differentiation of descent, effected through adjustment of various environments; and so on through the sphere of the sciences. In short, our conceptions attain a maximum of definite individuality and of generality (or applicability) in the degree to which they show how things depend upon one another or influence one another, instead of expressing the qualities that objects possess statically. The ideal of a system of scientific conceptions is to attain continuity, freedom, and flexibility of transition in passing from any fact and meaning to any other; this demand is met in the degree in which we lay hold of the dynamic ties that hold things together in a continuously changing process—a principle that states insight into mode of production or growth.

Chapter Ten

Concentrate and Abstract Thinking

False notions of concrete and abstract

The maxim enjoined upon teachers, "to proceed from the concrete to the abstract," is perhaps familiar rather than comprehended. Few who read and hear it gain a clear conception of the starting-point, the concrete; of the nature of the goal, the abstract; and of the exact nature of the path to be traversed in going from one to the other. At times the injunction is positively misunderstood, being taken to mean that education should advance from things to thought—as if any dealing with things in which thinking is not involved could possibly be educative. So understood, the maxim encourages mechanical routine or sensuous excitation at one end of the educational scale—the lower—and academic and unapplied learning at the upper end.

Actually, all dealing with things, even the child's, is immersed in inferences; things are clothed by the suggestions they arouse, and are significant as challenges to interpretation or as evidences to substantiate a belief. Nothing could be more unnatural than instruction in things without thought; in sense-perceptions without judgments based upon them. And if the abstract to which we are to proceed denotes thought apart from things, the goal recommended is formal and empty, for effective thought always refers, more or less directly, to things.

Direct and indirect understanding again

Yet the maxim has a meaning which, understood and supplemented, states the line of development of logical capacity. What is this signification? Concrete denotes a meaning definitely marked off from other meanings so that it is readily apprehended by itself. When we hear the words, table, chair, stove, coat, we do not have to reflect in order to grasp what is meant. The terms convey meaning so directly that no effort at translating is needed. The meanings of some terms and things, however, are grasped only by first calling to mind more familiar things and then tracing out connections between them and what we do not understand. Roughly speaking, the former kind of meanings is concrete; the latter abstract.

What is familiar is mentally concrete

To one who is thoroughly at home in physics and chemistry, the notions of atom and molecule are fairly concrete. They are constantly used without involving any labor of thought in apprehending what they mean. But the layman and the beginner in science have first to remind themselves of things with which they already are well acquainted, and go through a process of slow translation; the terms atom and molecule losing, moreover, their hard-won meaning only too easily if familiar things, and the line of transition from them to the strange, drop out of mind. The same difference is illustrated by any technical terms: coefficient and exponent in algebra, triangle and square in their geometric as distinct from their popular meanings; capital and value as used in political economy, and so on.

Practical things are familiar

The difference as noted is purely relative to the intellectual progress of an individual; what is abstract at one period of growth is concrete at another; or even the contrary, as one finds that things supposed to be thoroughly familiar involve strange factors and unsolved problems. There is, nevertheless, a general line of cleavage which, deciding upon the whole what things fall within the limits of familiar acquaintance and what without, marks off the concrete and the abstract in a more permanent way. These limits are fixed mainly by the demands of practical life. Things such as sticks and stones, meat and potatoes, houses and trees, are such constant features of the environment of which we have to take account in order to live, that their important meanings are soon learnt, and indissolubly associated with objects. We are acquainted with a thing (or it is familiar to us) when we have so much to do with it that its strange and unexpected corners are rubbed off. The necessities of social intercourse convey to adults a like concreteness upon such terms as taxes, elections, wages, the law, and so on. Things the meaning of which I personally do not take in directly, appliances of cook, carpenter, or weaver, for example, are nevertheless unhesitatingly classed as concrete, since they are so directly connected with our common social life.

The theoretical, or strictly intellectual, is abstract

By contrast, the abstract is the theoretical, or that not intimately associated with practical concerns. The abstract thinker (the man of pure science as he is sometimes called) deliberately abstracts from application in life; that is, he leaves practical uses out of account. This, however, is a merely negative statement. What remains when connections with use and application are excluded? Evidently only what has to do with knowing considered as an end in itself. Many notions of science are abstract, not only because they cannot be understood without a long apprenticeship in the science (which is equally true of technical matters in the arts), but also because the whole content of their meaning has been framed for the sole purpose of facilitating further knowledge, inquiry, and speculation. When thinking is used as a means to some end, good, or value beyond itself, it is concrete; when it is employed simply as a means to more thinking, it is abstract. To a theorist an idea is adequate and self-contained just because it engages and rewards thought; to a medical practitioner, an engineer, an artist, a merchant, a politician, it is complete only when employed in the furthering of some interest in life—health, wealth, beauty, goodness, success, or what you will.

Contempt for theory

For the great majority of men under ordinary circumstances, the practical exigencies of life are almost, if not quite, coercive. Their main business is the proper conduct of their affairs. Whatever is of significance only as affording scope for thinking is pallid and remote—almost artificial. Hence the contempt felt by the practical and successful executive for the "mere theorist"; hence his conviction that certain things may be all very well in theory, but that they will not do in practice; in general, the depreciatory way in which he uses the terms abstract, theoretical, and intellectual—as distinct from intelligent.

But theory is highly practical

This attitude is justified, of course, under certain conditions. But depreciation of theory does not contain the whole truth, as common or practical sense recognizes. There is such a thing, even from the common-sense standpoint, as being "too practical," as being so intent upon the immediately practical as not to see beyond the end of one's nose or as to cut off the limb upon which one is sitting. The question is one of limits, of degrees and adjustments, rather than one of absolute separation. Truly practical men give their minds free play about a subject without asking too closely at every point for the advantage to be gained; exclusive preoccupation with matters of use and application so narrows the horizon as in the long run to defeat itself. It does not pay to tether one's thoughts to the post of use with too short a rope. Power in action requires some largeness and imaginativeness of vision. Men must at least have enough interest in thinking for the sake of thinking to escape the limits of routine and custom. Interest in knowledge for the sake of knowledge, in thinking for the sake of the free play of thought, is necessary then to the emancipation of practical life—to make it rich and progressive.

We may now recur to the pedagogic maxim of going from the concrete to the abstract.

Begin with the concrete means begin with practical manipulations

1. Since the concrete denotes thinking applied to activities for the sake of dealing effectively with the difficulties that present themselves practically, "beginning with the concrete" signifies that we should at the outset make much of doing; especially, make much in occupations that are not of a routine and mechanical kind and hence require intelligent selection and adaptation of means and materials. We do not "follow the order of nature" when we multiply mere sensations or accumulate physical objects. Instruction in number is not concrete merely because splints or beans or dots are employed, while whenever the use and bearing of number relations are clearly perceived, the number idea is concrete even if figures alone are used. Just what sort of symbol it is best to use at a given time—whether blocks, or lines, or figures—is entirely a matter of adjustment to the given case. If physical things used in teaching number or geography or anything else do not leave the mind illuminated with recognition of a meaning beyond themselves, the instruction that uses them is as abstract as that which doles out ready-made definitions and rules; for it distracts attention from ideas to mere physical excitations.

Confusion of the concrete with the sensibly isolated

The conception that we have only to put before the senses particular physical objects in order to impress certain ideas upon the mind amounts almost to a superstition. The introduction of object lessons and sense-training scored a distinct advance over the prior method of linguistic symbols, and this advance tended to blind educators to the fact that only a halfway step had been taken. Things and sensations develop the child, indeed, but only because he uses them in mastering his body and in the scheme of his activities. Appropriate continuous occupations or activities involve the use of natural materials, tools, modes of energy, and do it in a way that compels thinking as to what they mean, how they are related to one another and to the realization of ends; while the mere isolated presentation of things remains barren and dead. A few generations ago the great obstacle in the way of reform of primary education was belief in the almost magical efficacy of the symbols of language (including number) to produce mental training; at present, belief in the efficacy of objects just as objects, blocks the way. As frequently happens, the better is an enemy of the best.

Transfer of interest to intellectual matters

2. The interest in results, in the successful carrying on of an activity, should be gradually transferred to study of objects—their properties, consequences, structures, causes, and effects. The adult when at work in his life calling is rarely free to devote time or energy—beyond the necessities of his immediate action—to the study of what he deals with. The educative activities of childhood should be so arranged that direct interest in the activity and its outcome create a demand for attention to matters that have a more and more indirect and remote connection with the original activity. The direct interest in carpentering or shop work should yield organically and gradually an interest in geometric and mechanical problems. The interest in cooking should grow into an interest in chemical experimentation and in the physiology and hygiene of bodily growth. The making of pictures should pass to an interest in the technique of representation and the æsthetics of appreciation, and so on. This development is what the term go signifies in the maxim "go from the concrete to the abstract"; it represents the dynamic and truly educative factor of the process.

Development of delight in the activity of thinking

3. The outcome, the abstract to which education is to proceed, is an

interest in intellectual matters for their own sake, a delight in thinking for the sake of thinking. It is an old story that acts and processes which at the outset are incidental to something else develop and maintain an absorbing value of their own. So it is with thinking and with knowledge; at first incidental to results and adjustments beyond themselves, they attract more and more attention to themselves till they become ends, not means. Children engage, unconstrainedly and continually, in reflective inspection and testing for the sake of what they are interested in doing successfully. Habits of thinking thus generated may increase in volume and extent till they become of importance on their own account.

Examples of the transition

The three instances cited in Chapter Six represented an ascending cycle from the practical to the theoretical. Taking thought to keep a personal engagement is obviously of the concrete kind. Endeavoring to work out the meaning of a certain part of a boat is an instance of an intermediate kind. The reason for the existence and position of the pole is a practical reason, so that to the architect the problem was purely concrete—the maintenance of a certain system of action. But for the passenger on the boat, the problem was theoretical, more or less speculative. It made no difference to his reaching his destination whether he worked out the meaning of the pole. The third case, that of the appearance and movement of the bubbles, illustrates a strictly theoretical or abstract case. No overcoming of physical obstacles, no adjustment of external means to ends, is at stake. Curiosity, intellectual curiosity, is challenged by a seemingly anomalous occurrence; and thinking tries simply to account for an apparent exception in terms of recognized principles.

Theoretical knowledge never the whole end

(i) Abstract thinking, it should be noted, represents an end, not the end. The power of sustained thinking on matters remote from direct use is an outgrowth of practical and immediate modes of thought, but not a substitute for them. The educational end is not the destruction of power to think so as to surmount obstacles and adjust means and ends; it is not its replacement by abstract reflection. Nor is theoretical thinking a higher type of thinking than practical. A person who has at command both types of thinking is of a higher order than he who possesses only one. Methods that in developing abstract intellectual abilities weaken habits of practical or concrete thinking, fall as much short of the educational ideal as do the methods that in cultivating ability to plan, to invent, to arrange, to forecast, fail to secure some delight in thinking irrespective of practical consequences.

Nor that most congenial to the majority of pupils

(ii) Educators should also note the very great individual differences that exist; they should not try to force one pattern and model upon all. In many (probably the majority) the executive tendency, the habit of mind that thinks for purposes of conduct and achievement, not for the sake of knowing, remains dominant to the end. Engineers, lawyers, doctors, merchants, are much more numerous in adult life than scholars, scientists, and philosophers. While education should strive to make men who, however prominent their professional interests and aims, partake of the spirit of the scholar, philosopher, and scientist, no good reason appears why education should esteem the one mental habit inherently superior to the other, and deliberately try to transform the type from practical to theoretical. Have not our schools been one-sidedly devoted to the more abstract type of thinking, thus doing injustice to the majority of pupils? Has not the idea of a "liberal" and "humane" education tended too often in practice to the production of technical, because overspecialized, thinkers?

Aim of education is a working balance

The aim of education should be to secure a balanced interaction of the two types of mental attitude, having sufficient regard to the disposition of the individual not to hamper and cripple whatever powers are naturally strong in him. The narrowness of individuals of strong concrete bent needs to be liberalized. Every opportunity that occurs within their practical activities for developing curiosity and susceptibility to intellectual problems should be seized. Violence is not done to natural disposition, but the latter is broadened. As regards the smaller number of those who have a taste for abstract, purely intellectual topics, pains should be taken to multiply opportunities and demands for the application of ideas; for translating symbolic truths into terms of social life and its ends. Every human being has both capabilities, and every individual will be more effective and happier if both powers are developed in easy and close interaction with each other.

Chapter Eleven

Empirical and Scientific Thinking

§ 1. Empirical Thinking

Empirical thinking depends on past habits

Apart from the development of scientific method, inferences depend upon habits that have been built up under the influence of a number of particular experiences not themselves arranged for logical purposes. A says, "It will probably rain to-morrow." B asks, "Why do you think so?" and A replies, "Because the sky was lowering at sunset." When B asks, "What has that to do with it?" A responds, "I do not know, but it generally does rain after such a sunset." He does not perceive any connection between the appearance of the sky and coming rain; he is not aware of any continuity in the facts themselves—any law or principle, as we usually say. He simply, from frequently recurring conjunctions of the events, has associated them so that when he sees one he thinks of the other. One suggests the other, or is associated with it. A man may believe it will rain to-morrow because he has consulted the barometer; but if he has no conception how the height of the mercury column (or the position of an index moved by its rise and fall) is connected with variations of atmospheric pressure, and how these in turn are connected with the amount of moisture in the air, his belief in the likelihood of rain is purely empirical. When men lived in the open and got their living by hunting, fishing, or pasturing flocks, the detection of the signs and indications of weather changes was a matter of great importance. A body of proverbs and maxims, forming an extensive section of traditionary folklore, was developed. But as long as there was no understanding why or how certain events were signs, as long as foresight and weather shrewdness rested simply upon repeated conjunction among facts, beliefs about the weather were thoroughly empirical.

It is fairly adequate in some matters

In similar fashion learned men in the Orient learned to predict, with considerable accuracy, the recurrent positions of the planets, the sun and the moon, and to foretell the time of eclipses, without understanding in any degree the laws of the movements of heavenly bodies—that is, without having a notion of the continuities existing among the facts themselves. They had learned from repeated observations that things happened in about such and such a fashion. Till a comparatively recent time, the truths of medicine were mainly in the same condition. Experience had shown that "upon the whole," "as a rule," "generally or usually speaking," certain results followed certain remedies, when symptoms were given. Our beliefs about human nature in individuals (psychology) and in masses (sociology) are still very largely of a purely empirical sort. Even the science of geometry, now frequently reckoned a typical rational science, began, among the Egyptians, as an accumulation of recorded observations about methods of approximate mensuration of land surfaces; and only gradually assumed, among the Greeks, scientific form.

The disadvantages of purely empirical thinking are obvious.

But is very apt to lead to false beliefs

1. While many empirical conclusions are, roughly speaking, correct; while they are exact enough to be of great help in practical life; while the presages of a weatherwise sailor or hunter may be more accurate, within a certain restricted range, than those of a scientist who relies wholly upon scientific observations and tests; while, indeed, empirical observations and records furnish the raw or crude material of scientific knowledge, yet the empirical method affords no way of discriminating between right and wrong conclusions. Hence it is responsible for a multitude of false beliefs. The technical designation for one of the commonest fallacies is post hoc, ergo propter hoc; the belief that because one thing comes after another, it comes because of the other. Now this fallacy of method is the animating principle of empirical conclusions, even when correct—the correctness being almost as much a matter of good luck as of method. That potatoes should be planted only during the crescent moon, that near the sea people are born at high tide and die at low tide, that a comet is an omen of danger, that bad luck follows the cracking of a mirror, that

a patent medicine cures a disease—these and a thousand like notions are asseverated on the basis of empirical coincidence and conjunction. Moreover, habits of expectation and belief are formed otherwise than by a number of repeated similar cases.

And does not enable us to cope with the novel

2. The more numerous the experienced instances and the closer the watch kept upon them, the greater is the trustworthiness of constant conjunction as evidence of connection among the things themselves. Many of our most important beliefs still have only this sort of warrant. No one can yet tell, with certainty, the necessary cause of old age or of death—which are empirically the most certain of all expectations. But even the most reliable beliefs of this type fail when they confront the novel. Since they rest upon past uniformities, they are useless when further experience departs in any considerable measure from ancient incident and wonted precedent. Empirical inference follows the grooves and ruts that custom wears, and has no track to follow when the groove disappears. So important is this aspect of the matter that Clifford found the difference between ordinary skill and scientific thought right here. "Skill enables a man to deal with the same circumstances that he has met before, scientific thought enables him to deal with different circumstances that he has never met before." And he goes so far as to define scientific thinking as "the application of old experience to new circumstances."

And leads to laziness and presumption

3. We have not yet made the acquaintance of the most harmful feature of the empirical method. Mental inertia, laziness, unjustifiable conservatism, are its probable accompaniments. Its general effect upon mental attitude is more serious than even the specific wrong conclusions in which it has landed. Wherever the chief dependence in forming inferences is upon the conjunctions observed in past experience, failures to agree with the usual order are slurred over, cases of successful confirmation are exaggerated. Since the mind naturally demands some principle of continuity, some connecting link between separate facts and causes, forces are arbitrarily invented for that purpose. Fantastic and mythological explanations are resorted to in order to supply missing

links. The pump brings water because nature abhors a vacuum; opium makes men sleep because it has a dormitive potency; we recollect a past event because we have a faculty of memory. In the history of the progress of human knowledge, out and out myths accompany the first stage of empiricism; while "hidden essences" and "occult forces" mark its second stage. By their very nature, these "causes" escape observation, so that their explanatory value can be neither confirmed nor refuted by further observation or experience. Hence belief in them becomes purely traditionary. They give rise to doctrines which, inculcated and handed down, become dogmas; subsequent inquiry and reflection are actually stifled.

And to dogmatism

Certain men or classes of men come to be the accepted guardians and transmitters—instructors—of established doctrines. To question the beliefs is to question their authority; to accept the beliefs is evidence of loyalty to the powers that be, a proof of good citizenship. Passivity, docility, acquiescence, come to be primal intellectual virtues. Facts and events presenting novelty and variety are slighted, or are sheared down till they fit into the Procrustean bed of habitual belief. Inquiry and doubt are silenced by citation of ancient laws or a multitude of miscellaneous and unsifted cases. This attitude of mind generates dislike of change, and the resulting aversion to novelty is fatal to progress. What will not fit into the established canons is outlawed; men who make new discoveries are objects of suspicion and even of persecution. Beliefs that perhaps originally were the products of fairly extensive and careful observation are stereotyped into fixed traditions and semi-sacred dogmas accepted simply upon authority, and are mixed with fantastic conceptions that happen to have won the acceptance of authorities.

§ 2. Scientific Method

Scientific thinking analyzes the present case

In contrast with the empirical method stands the scientific. Scientific method replaces the repeated conjunction or coincidence of separate facts by discovery of a single comprehensive fact, effecting this replacement by breaking up the coarse or gross facts of observation into a number of minuter processes not directly accessible to perception.

Illustration from suction of empirical method

If a layman were asked why water rises from the cistern when an ordinary pump is worked, he would doubtless answer, "By suction." Suction is regarded as a force like heat or pressure. If such a person is confronted by the fact that water rises with a suction pump only about thirty-three feet, he easily disposes of the difficulty on the ground that all forces vary in their intensities and finally reach a limit at which they cease to operate. The variation with elevation above the sea level of the height to which water can be pumped is either unnoticed, or, if noted, is dismissed as one of the curious anomalies in which nature abounds.

Of scientific method

Relies on differences

Now the scientist advances by assuming that what seems to observation to be a single total fact is in truth complex. He attempts, therefore, to break up the single fact of water-rising-in-the-pipe into a number of lesser facts. His method of proceeding is by varying conditions one by one so far as possible, and noting just what happens when a given condition is eliminated. There are two methods for varying conditions. The first is an extension of the empirical method of observation. It consists in comparing very carefully the results of a great number of observations which have occurred under accidentally different conditions. The difference in the rise of the water at different heights above the sea level, and its total cessation when the distance to be lifted is, even at sea level, more than thirty-three feet, are emphasized, instead of being slurred over. The purpose is to find out what special conditions are present when the effect occurs and absent when it fails to occur. These special conditions are then substituted for the gross fact, or regarded as its principle—the key to understanding it.

And creates differences

The method of analysis by comparing cases is, however, badly handicapped; it can do nothing until it is presented with a certain number of diversified cases. And even when different cases are at hand, it will be questionable whether they vary in just these respects in which it is important that they should vary in order to throw light upon the question at issue. The method is passive and dependent upon external accidents. Hence the superiority of the active or experimental method. Even a small number of observations may suggest an explanation—a hypothesis or theory. Working upon this suggestion, the scientist may then intentionally vary conditions and note what happens. If the empirical observations have suggested to him the possibility of a connection between air pressure on the water and the rising of the water in the tube where air pressure is absent, he deliberately empties the air out of the vessel in which the water is contained and notes that suction no longer works; or he intentionally increases atmospheric pressure on the water and notes the result. He institutes experiments to calculate the weight of air at the sea level and at various levels above, and compares the results of reasoning based upon the pressure of air of these various weights upon a certain volume of water with the results actually obtained by observation. Observations formed by variation of conditions on the basis of some idea or theory constitute experiment. Experiment is the chief resource in scientific reasoning because it facilitates the picking out of significant elements in a gross, vague whole.

Analysis and synthesis again

Experimental thinking, or scientific reasoning, is thus a conjoint process of analysis and synthesis, or, in less technical language, of discrimination and assimilation or identification. The gross fact of water rising when the suction valve is worked is resolved or discriminated into a number of independent variables, some of which had never before been observed or even thought of in connection with the fact. One of these facts, the weight of the atmosphere, is then selectively seized upon as the key to the entire phenomenon. This disentangling constitutes analysis. But atmosphere and its pressure or weight is a fact not confined to this single instance. It is a fact familiar or at least discoverable as operative in a great number of other events. In fixing upon this imperceptible and minute fact as the essence or key to the elevation of water by the pump, the pump-fact has thus been assimilated to a whole group of ordinary facts from which it was previously isolated. This assimilation constitutes synthesis. Moreover, the fact of atmospheric pressure is itself a case of one of the commonest of all facts—weight or gravitational force. Conclusions that apply to the common fact of weight are thus transferable to the consideration and interpretation of the relatively rare and exceptional case of the suction of water. The suction pump is seen to be a case of the same kind or sort as the siphon, the barometer, the rising of the balloon, and a multitude of other things with which at first sight it has no connection at all. This is another instance of the synthetic or assimilative phase of scientific thinking.

If we revert to the advantages of scientific over empirical thinking, we find that we now have the clue to them.

Lessened liability to error

(a) The increased security, the added factor of certainty or proof, is due to the substitution of the detailed and specific fact of atmospheric pressure for the gross and total and relatively miscellaneous fact of suction. The latter is complex, and its complexity is due to many unknown and unspecified factors; hence, any statement about it is more or less random, and likely to be defeated by any unforeseen variation of circumstances. Comparatively, at least, the minute and detailed fact of air pressure is a measurable and definite fact—one that can be picked out and managed with assurance.

Ability to manage the new

(b) As analysis accounts for the added certainty, so synthesis accounts for ability to cope with the novel and variable. Weight is a much commoner fact than atmospheric weight, and this in turn is a much commoner fact than the workings of the suction pump. To be able to substitute the common and frequent fact for that which is relatively rare and peculiar is to reduce the seemingly novel and exceptional to cases of a general and familiar principle, and thus to bring them under control for interpretation and prediction.

As Professor James says: "Think of heat as motion and whatever is true of motion will be true of heat; but we have a hundred experiences of motion for every one of heat. Think of rays passing through this lens as cases of bending toward the perpendicular, and you substitute for the comparatively unfamiliar lens the very familiar notion of a particular change in direction of a line, of which notion every day brings us countless examples."

Interest in the future or in progress

(c) The change of attitude from conservative reliance upon the past, upon routine and custom, to faith in progress through the intelligent regulation of existing conditions, is, of course, the reflex of the scientific method of experimentation. The empirical method inevitably magnifies the influences of the past; the experimental method throws into relief the possibilities of the future. The empirical method says, "Wait till there is a sufficient number of cases" the experimental method says, "Produce the cases." The former depends upon nature's accidentally happening to present us with certain conjunctions of circumstances; the latter deliberately and intentionally endeavors to bring about the conjunction. By this method the notion of progress secures scientific warrant.

Physical versus logical force

Ordinary experience is controlled largely by the direct strength and intensity of various occurrences. What is bright, sudden, loud, secures notice and is given a conspicuous rating. What is dim, feeble, and continuous gets ignored, or is regarded as of slight importance. Customary experience tends to, the control of thinking by considerations of direct and immediate strength rather than by those of importance in the long run. Animals without the power of forecast and planning must, upon the whole, respond to the stimuli that are most urgent at the moment, or cease to exist. These stimuli lose nothing of their direct urgency and clamorous insistency when the thinking power develops; and yet thinking demands the subordination of the immediate stimulus to the remote and distant. The feeble and the minute may be of much greater importance than the glaring and the big. The latter may be signs of a force that is already exhausting itself; the former may indicate the beginnings of a process in which the whole fortune of the individual is involved. The prime necessity for scientific thought is that the thinker be freed from the tyranny of sense stimuli and habit, and this emancipation is also the necessary condition of progress.

Illustration from moving water

Consider the following quotation: "When it first occurred to a reflecting mind that moving water had a property identical with human or brute force, namely, the property of setting other masses in motion, overcoming inertia and resistance,—when the sight of the stream suggested through this point of likeness the power of the animal,—a new addition was made to the class of prime movers, and when circumstances permitted, this power could become a substitute for the others. It may seem to the modern understanding, familiar with water wheels and drifting rafts, that the similarity here was an extremely obvious one. But if we put ourselves back into an early state of mind, when running water affected the mind by its brilliancy, its roar and irregular devastation, we may easily suppose that to identify this with animal muscular energy was by no means an obvious effort."

Value of abstraction

If we add to these obvious sensory features the various social customs and expectations which fix the attitude of the individual, the evil of the subjection of free and fertile suggestion to empirical considerations becomes clear. A certain power of abstraction, of deliberate turning away from the habitual responses to a situation, was required before men could be emancipated to follow up suggestions that in the end are fruitful.

Experience as inclusive of thought

In short, the term experience may be interpreted either with reference to the empirical or the experimental attitude of mind. Experience is not a rigid and closed thing; it is vital, and hence growing. When dominated by the past, by custom and routine, it is often opposed to the reasonable, the thoughtful. But experience also includes the reflection that sets us free from the limiting influence of sense, appetite, and tradition. Experience may welcome and assimilate all that the most exact and penetrating thought discovers. Indeed, the business of education might be defined as just such an emancipation and enlargement of experience. Education takes the individual while he is relatively plastic, before he has become so indurated by isolated experiences as to be rendered hopelessly empirical in his habit of mind. The attitude of childhood is naïve, wondering, experimental; the world of man and nature is new. Right methods of education preserve and perfect this attitude, and thereby short-circuit for the individual the slow progress of the race, eliminating the waste that comes from inert routine.

PART THREE

The Training of Thought

Chapter Twelve

Activity and the Training of Thought

In this chapter we shall gather together and amplify considerations that have already been advanced, in various passages of the preceding pages, concerning the relation of action to thought. We shall follow, though not with exactness, the order of development in the unfolding human being.

§ 1. The Early Stage of Activity

1. The baby's problem determines his thinking

The sight of a baby often calls out the question: "What do you suppose he is thinking about?" By the nature of the case, the question is unanswerable in detail; but, also by the nature of the case, we may be sure about a baby's chief interest. His primary problem is mastery of his body as a tool of securing comfortable and effective adjustments to his surroundings, physical and social. The child has to learn to do almost everything: to see, to hear, to reach, to handle, to balance the body, to creep, to walk, and so on. Even if it be true that human beings have even more instinctive reactions than lower animals, it is also true that instinctive tendencies are much less perfect in men, and that most of them are of little use till they are intelligently combined and directed. A little chick just out of the shell will after a few trials peck at and grasp grains of food with its beak as well as at any later time. This involves a complicated coördination of the eye and the head. An infant does not even begin to reach definitely for things that the eye sees till he is several months old, and even then several weeks' practice is required before he learns the adjustment so as neither to overreach nor to underreach. It may not be literally true that the child will grasp for the moon, but it is true that he needs much practice before he can tell whether an object is within reach or not. The arm is thrust out instinctively in response to a stimulus from the eye, and this tendency is the origin of the ability to reach and grasp exactly and quickly; but nevertheless final mastery requires observing and selecting the successful movements, and arranging them in view of an end. These operations of conscious selection and arrangement constitute thinking, though of a rudimentary type.

Mastery of the body is an intellectual problem

Since mastery of the bodily organs is necessary for all later developments, such problems are both interesting and important, and solving them supplies a very genuine training of thinking power. The joy the child shows in learning to use his limbs, to translate what he sees into what he handles, to connect sounds with sights, sights with taste and touch, and the rapidity with which intelligence grows in the first year and a half of life (the time during which the more fundamental problems of the use of the organism are mastered), are sufficient evidence that the development of physical control is not a physical but an intellectual achievement.

2. The problem of social adjustment and intercourse

Although in the early months the child is mainly occupied in learning to use his body to accommodate himself to physical conditions in a comfortable way and to use things skillfully and effectively, yet social adjustments are very important. In connection with parents, nurse, brother, and sister, the child learns the signs of satisfaction of hunger, of removal of discomfort, of the approach of agreeable light, color, sound, and so on. His contact with physical things is regulated by persons, and he soon distinguishes persons as the most important and interesting of all the objects with which he has to do. Speech, the accurate adaptation of sounds heard to the movements of tongue and lips, is, however, the great instrument of social adaptation; and with the development of speech (usually in the second year) adaptation of the baby's activities to and with those of other persons gives the keynote of mental life. His range of possible activities is indefinitely widened as he watches what other persons do, and as he tries to understand and to do what they encourage him to attempt. The outline pattern of mental life is thus set in the first four or five years. Years, centuries, generations of invention and planning, may have gone to the development of the performances and occupations of the adults surrounding the child. Yet for him their activities are direct stimuli; they are part of his natural environment; they are carried on in physical terms that appeal to his eye, ear, and touch. He cannot, of course, appropriate their meaning directly through his senses; but they furnish stimuli to which he responds, so that his attention is focussed upon a higher order of materials and of problems. Were it not for this process by which the achievements of one generation form the stimuli that direct the activities of the next, the story of civilization would be writ in water, and each generation would have laboriously to make for itself, if it could, its way out of savagery.

Social adjustment results in imitation but is not caused by it

Imitation is one of the means by which the activities of adults supply stimuli which are so interesting, so varied, so complex, and so novel, as to occasion a rapid progress of thought. Mere imitation, however, would not give rise to thinking; if we could learn like parrots by simply copying the outward acts of others, we should never have to think; nor should we know, after we had mastered the copied act, what was the meaning of the thing we had done. Educators (and psychologists) have often assumed that acts which reproduce the behavior of others are acquired merely by imitation. But a child rarely learns by conscious imitation; and to say that his imitation is unconscious is to say that it is not from his standpoint imitation at all. The word, the gesture, the act, the occupation of another, falls in line with some impulse already active and suggests some satisfactory mode of expression, some end in which it may find fulfillment. Having this end of his own, the child then notes other persons, as he notes natural events, to get further suggestions as to means of its realization. He selects some of the means he observes, tries them on, finds them successful or unsuccessful, is confirmed or weakened in his belief in their value, and so continues selecting, arranging, adapting, testing, till he can accomplish what he wishes. The onlooker may then observe the resemblance of this act to some act of an adult, and conclude that it was acquired by imitation, while as a matter of fact it was acquired by attention, observation, selection, experimentation, and confirmation by results. Only because this method is employed is there intellectual discipline and an educative result. The presence of adult activities plays an enormous rôle in the intellectual growth of the child because they add to the natural stimuli of the world new stimuli which are more exactly adapted to the needs of a human being, which are richer, better organized, more complex in range, permitting more flexible adaptations, and calling out novel reactions. But in utilizing these stimuli the child follows the same methods that he uses when he is forced to think in order to master his body.

§ 2. Play, Work, and Allied Forms of Activity

Play indicates the domination of activity by meanings or ideas

Organization of ideas involved in play

When things become signs, when they gain a representative capacity as standing for other things, play is transformed from mere physical exuberance into an activity involving a mental factor. A little girl who had broken her doll was seen to perform with the leg of the doll all the operations of washing, putting to bed, and fondling, that she had been accustomed to perform with the entire doll. The part stood for the whole; she reacted not to the stimulus sensibly present, but to the meaning suggested by the sense object. So children use a stone for a table, leaves for plates, acorns for cups. So they use their dolls, their trains, their blocks, their other toys. In manipulating them, they are living not with the physical things, but in the large world of meanings, natural and social, evoked by these things. So when children play horse, play store, play house or making calls, they are subordinating the physically present to the ideally signified. In this way, a world of meanings, a store of concepts (so fundamental to all intellectual achievement), is defined and built up. Moreover, not only do meanings thus become familiar acquaintances, but they are organized, arranged in groups, made to cohere in connected ways. A play and a story blend insensibly into each other. The most fanciful plays of children rarely lose all touch with the mutual fitness and pertinency of various meanings to one another; the "freest" plays observe some principles of coherence and unification. They have a beginning, middle, and end. In games, rules of order run through various minor acts and bind them into a connected whole. The rhythm, the competition, and coöperation involved in most plays and games also introduce organization. There is, then, nothing mysterious or mystical in the discovery made by Plato and remade by Froebel that play is the chief, almost the only, mode of education for the child in the years of later infancy.

The playful attitude

Playfulness is a more important consideration than play. The former is an attitude of mind; the latter is a passing outward manifestation of this attitude. When things are treated simply as vehicles of suggestion, what is suggested overrides the thing. Hence the playful attitude is one of freedom. The person is not bound to the physical traits of things, nor does he care whether a thing really means (as we say) what he takes it to represent. When the child plays horse with a broom and cars with chairs, the fact that the broom does not really represent a horse, or a chair a locomotive, is of no account. In order, then, that playfulness may not terminate in arbitrary fancifulness and in building up an imaginary world alongside the world of actual things, it is necessary that the play attitude should gradually pass into a work attitude.

The work attitude is interested in means and ends

What is work—work not as mere external performance, but as attitude of mind? It signifies that the person is not content longer to accept and to act upon the meanings that things suggest, but demands congruity of meaning with the things themselves. In the natural course of growth, children come to find irresponsible make-believe plays inadequate. A fiction is too easy a way out to afford content. There is not enough stimulus to call forth satisfactory mental response. When this point is reached, the ideas that things suggest must be applied to the things with some regard to fitness. A small cart, resembling a "real" cart, with "real" wheels, tongue, and body, meets the mental demand better than merely making believe that anything which comes to hand is a cart. Occasionally to take part in setting a "real" table with "real" dishes brings more reward than forever to make believe a flat stone is a table and that leaves are dishes. The interest may still center in the meanings, the things may be of importance only as amplifying a certain meaning. So far the attitude is one of play. But the meaning is now of such a character that it must find appropriate embodiment in actual things.

The dictionary does not permit us to call such activities work. Nevertheless, they represent a genuine passage of play into work. For work (as a mental attitude, not as mere external performance) means interest in the adequate embodiment of a meaning (a suggestion, purpose, aim) in objective form through the use of appropriate materials and appliances. Such an attitude takes advantage of the meanings aroused and built up in free play, but controls their development by seeing to it that they are applied to things in ways consistent with the observable structure of the things themselves.

And in processes on account of their results

The point of this distinction between play and work may be cleared up by comparing it with a more usual way of stating the difference. In play activity, it is said, the interest is in the activity for its own sake; in work, it is in the product or result in which the activity terminates. Hence the former is purely free, while the latter is tied down by the end to be achieved. When the difference is stated in this sharp fashion, there is almost always introduced a false, unnatural separation between process and product, between activity and its achieved outcome. The true distinction is not between an interest in activity for its own sake and interest in the external result of that activity, but between an interest in an activity just as it flows on from moment to moment, and an interest in an activity as tending to a culmination, to an outcome, and therefore possessing a thread of continuity binding together its successive stages. Both may equally exemplify interest in an activity "for its own sake"; but in one case the activity in which the interest resides is more or less casual, following the accident of circumstance and whim, or of dictation; in the other, the activity is enriched by the sense that it leads somewhere, that it amounts to something.

Consequences of the sharp separation of play and work

Were it not that the false theory of the relation of the play and the work attitudes has been connected with unfortunate modes of school practice, insistence upon a truer view might seem an unnecessary refinement. But the sharp break that unfortunately prevails between the kindergarten and the grades is evidence that the theoretical distinction has practical implications. Under the title of play, the former is rendered unduly symbolic, fanciful, sentimental, and arbitrary; while under the antithetical caption of work the latter contains many tasks externally assigned. The former has no end and the latter an end so remote that only the educator, not the child, is aware that it is an end.

There comes a time when children must extend and make more exact their acquaintance with existing things; must conceive ends and consequences with sufficient definiteness to guide their actions by them, and must acquire some technical skill in selecting and arranging means to realize these ends. Unless these factors are gradually introduced in the earlier play period, they must be introduced later abruptly and arbitrarily, to the manifest disadvantage of both the earlier and the later stages.

False notions of imagination and utility

The sharp opposition of play and work is usually associated with false notions of utility and imagination. Activity that is directed upon matters of home and neighborhood interest is depreciated as merely utilitarian. To let the child wash dishes, set the table, engage in cooking, cut and sew dolls' clothes, make boxes that will hold "real things," and construct his own playthings by using hammer and nails, excludes, so it is said, the æsthetic and appreciative factor, eliminates imagination, and subjects the child's development to material and practical concerns; while (so it is said) to reproduce symbolically the domestic relationships of birds and other animals, of human father and mother and child, of workman and tradesman, of knight, soldier, and magistrate, secures a liberal exercise of mind, of great moral as well as intellectual value. It has been even stated that it is over-physical and utilitarian if a child plants seeds and takes care of growing plants in the kindergarten; while reproducing dramatically operations of planting, cultivating, reaping, and so on, either with no physical materials or with symbolic representatives, is highly educative to the imagination and to spiritual appreciation. Toy dolls, trains of cars, boats, and engines are rigidly excluded, and the employ of cubes, balls, and other symbols for representing these social activities is recommended on the same ground. The more unfitted the physical object for its imagined purpose, such as a cube for a boat, the greater is the supposed appeal to the imagination.

Imagination a medium of realizing the absent and significant

There are several fallacies in this way of thinking. (a) The healthy imagination deals not with the unreal, but with the mental realization of what is suggested. Its exercise is not a flight into the purely fanciful and ideal, but a method of expanding and filling in what is real. To the child the homely activities going on about him are not utilitarian devices for accomplishing physical ends; they exemplify a wonderful world the depths of which he has not sounded, a world full of the mystery and promise that attend all the doings of the grown-ups whom he admires. However prosaic this world may be to the adults who find its duties routine affairs, to the child it is fraught with social meaning. To engage in it is to exercise the imagination in constructing an experience of wider value than any the child has yet mastered.

Only the already experienced can be symbolized

(b) Educators sometimes think children are reacting to a great moral or spiritual truth when the children's reactions are largely physical and sensational. Children have great powers of dramatic simulation, and their physical bearing may seem (to adults prepossessed with a philosophic theory) to indicate they have been impressed with some lesson of chivalry, devotion, or nobility, when the children themselves are occupied only with transitory physical excitations. To symbolize great truths far beyond the child's range of actual experience is an impossibility, and to attempt it is to invite love of momentary stimulation.

Useful work is not necessarily labor

(c) Just as the opponents of play in education always conceive of play as mere amusement, so the opponents of direct and useful activities confuse occupation with labor. The adult is acquainted with responsible labor upon which serious financial results depend. Consequently he seeks relief, relaxation, amusement. Unless children have prematurely worked for hire, unless they have come under the blight of child labor, no such division exists for them. Whatever appeals to them at all, appeals directly on its own account. There is no contrast between doing things for utility and for fun. Their life is more united and more wholesome. To suppose that activities customarily performed by adults only under the pressure of utility may not be done perfectly freely and joyously by children indicates a lack of imagination. Not the thing done but the quality of mind that goes into the doing settles what is utilitarian and what is unconstrained and educative.

§ 3. Constructive Occupations

The historic growth of sciences out of occupations

The history of culture shows that mankind's scientific knowledge and technical abilities have developed, especially in all their earlier stages, out of the fundamental problems of life. Anatomy and physiology grew out of the practical needs of keeping healthy and active; geometry and mechanics out of demands for measuring land, for building, and for making labor-saving machines; astronomy has been closely connected with navigation, keeping record of the passage of time; botany grew out of the requirements of medicine and of agronomy; chemistry has been associated with dyeing, metallurgy, and other industrial pursuits. In turn, modern industry is almost wholly a matter of applied science; year by year the domain of routine and crude empiricism is narrowed by the translation of scientific discovery into industrial invention. The trolley, the telephone, the electric light, the steam engine, with all their revolutionary consequences for social intercourse and control, are the fruits of science.

The intellectual possibilities of school occupations

These facts are full of educational significance. Most children are preëminently active in their tendencies. The schools have also taken on—largely from utilitarian, rather than from strictly educative reasons—a large number of active pursuits commonly grouped under the head of manual training, including also school gardens, excursions, and various graphic arts. Perhaps the most pressing problem of education at the present moment is to organize and relate these subjects so that they will become instruments for forming alert, persistent, and fruitful intellectual habits. That they take hold of the more primary and native equipment of children (appealing to their desire to do) is generally recognized; that they afford great opportunity for training in self-reliant and efficient social service is gaining acknowledgment. But they may also be used for presenting typical problems to be solved by personal reflection and experimentation, and by acquiring definite bodies of knowledge leading later to more specialized scientific knowledge. There is indeed no magic by which mere physical activity or deft manipulation will secure intellectual results. Manual subjects may be taught by routine, by dictation, or by convention as readily as bookish subjects. But intelligent consecutive work in gardening, cooking, or weaving, or in elementary wood and iron, may be planned which will inevitably result in students not only amassing information of practical and scientific importance in botany, zoölogy, chemistry, physics, and other sciences, but (what is more significant) in their becoming versed in methods of experimental inquiry and proof.

Reorganization of the course of study

That the elementary curriculum is overloaded is a common complaint. The only alternative to a reactionary return to the educational traditions of the past lies in working out the intellectual possibilities resident in the various arts, crafts, and occupations, and reorganizing the curriculum accordingly. Here, more than elsewhere, are found the means by which the blind and routine experience of the race may be transformed into illuminated and emancipated experiment.

Chapter Thirteen

Language and the Training of Thought

§ 1. Language as the Tool of Thinking

Ambiguous position of language

Speech has such a peculiarly intimate connection with thought as to require special discussion. Although the very word logic comes from logos, meaning indifferently both word or speech, and thought or reason, yet "words, words, words" denote intellectual barrenness, a sham of thought. Although schooling has language as its chief instrument (and often as its chief matter) of study, educational reformers have for centuries brought their severest indictments against the current use of language in the schools. The conviction that language is necessary to thinking (is even identical with it) is met by the contention that language perverts and conceals thought.

Language a necessary tool of thinking, for it alone fixes meanings

Three typical views have been maintained regarding the relation of thought and language: first, that they are identical; second, that words are the garb or clothing of thought, necessary not for thought but only for conveying it; and third (the view we shall here maintain) that while language is not thought it is necessary for thinking as well as for its communication. When it is said, however, that thinking is impossible without language, we must recall that language includes much more than oral and written speech. Gestures, pictures, monuments, visual images, finger movements—anything consciously employed as a sign is, logically, language. To say that language is necessary for thinking is to say that signs are necessary. Thought deals not with bare things, but with their meanings, their suggestions; and meanings, in order to be apprehended, must be embodied in sensible and particular existences.

Without meaning, things are nothing but blind stimuli or chance sources of pleasure and pain; and since meanings are not themselves tangible things, they must be anchored by attachment to some physical existence. Existences that are especially set aside to fixate and convey meanings are signs or symbols. If a man moves toward another to throw him out of the room, his movement is not a sign. If, however, the man points to the door with his hand, or utters the sound go, his movement is reduced to a vehicle of meaning: it is a sign or symbol. In the case of signs we care nothing for what they are in themselves, but everything for what they signify and represent. Canis, hund, chien, dog—it makes no difference what the outward thing is, so long as the meaning is presented.

Limitations of natural symbols

Natural objects are signs of other things and events. Clouds stand for rain; a footprint represents game or an enemy; a projecting rock serves to indicate minerals below the surface. The limitations of natural signs are, however, great. (i) The physical or direct sense excitation tends to distract attention from what is meant or indicated. Almost every one will recall pointing out to a kitten or puppy some object of food, only to have the animal devote himself to the hand pointing, not to the thing pointed at. (ii) Where natural signs alone exist, we are mainly at the mercy of external happenings; we have to wait until the natural event presents itself in order to be warned or advised of the possibility of some other event. (iii) Natural signs, not being originally intended to be signs, are cumbrous, bulky, inconvenient, unmanageable.

Artificial signs overcome these restrictions.

It is therefore indispensable for any high development of thought that there should be also intentional signs. Speech supplies the requirement. Gestures, sounds, written or printed forms, are strictly physical existences, but their native value is intentionally subordinated to the value they acquire as representative of meanings. (i) The direct and sensible value of faint sounds and minute written or printed marks is very slight. Accordingly, attention is not distracted from their representative function. (ii) Their production is under our direct control so that they may be produced when needed. When we can make the word rain, we do not have to wait for some physical forerunner of rain to call our thoughts in that direction. We cannot make the cloud; we can make the sound, and as a token of meaning the sound serves the purpose as well as the cloud. (iii) Arbitrary linguistic signs are convenient and easy to manage. They are compact, portable, and delicate. As long as we live we breathe; and modifications by the muscles of throat and mouth of the volume and quality of the air are simple, easy, and indefinitely controllable. Bodily postures and gestures of the hand and arm are also employed as signs, but they are coarse and unmanageable compared with modifications of breath to produce sounds. No wonder that oral speech has been selected as the main stuff of intentional intellectual signs. Sounds, while subtle, refined, and easily modifiable, are transitory. This defect is met by the system of written and printed words, appealing to the eye.

Bearing in mind the intimate connection of meanings and signs (or language), we may note in more detail what language does (1) for specific meanings, and (2) for the organization of meanings.

I. Individual Meanings. A verbal sign (a) selects, detaches, a meaning from what is otherwise a vague flux and blur; (b) it retains, registers, stores that meaning; and (c) applies it, when needed, to the comprehension of other things. Combining these various functions in a mixture of metaphors, we may say that a linguistic sign is a fence, a label, and a vehicle—all in one.

A sign makes a meaning distinct

(a) Every one has experienced how learning an appropriate name for what was dim and vague cleared up and crystallized the whole matter. Some meaning seems almost within reach, but is elusive; it refuses to condense into definite form; the attaching of a word somehow (just how, it is almost impossible to say) puts limits around the meaning, draws it out from the void, makes it stand out as an entity on its own account. When Emerson said that he would almost rather know the true name, the poet's name, for a thing, than to know the thing itself, he presumably had this irradiating and illuminating function of language in mind. The delight that children take in demanding and learning the names of everything about them indicates that meanings are becoming concrete individuals to them, so that their commerce with things is passing from the physical to the intellectual plane. It is hardly surprising that savages attach a magic efficacy to words. To name anything is to give it a title; to dignify and honor it by raising it from a mere physical occurrence to a meaning that is distinct and permanent. To know the names of people and things and to be able to manipulate these names is, in savage lore, to be in possession of their dignity and worth, to master them.

A sign preserves a meaning

(b) Things come and go; or we come and go, and either way things escape our notice. Our direct sensible relation to things is very limited. The suggestion of meanings by natural signs is limited to occasions of direct contact or vision. But a meaning fixed by a linguistic sign is conserved for future use. Even if the thing is not there to represent the meaning, the word may be produced so as to evoke the meaning. Since intellectual life depends on possession of a store of meanings, the importance of language as a tool of preserving meanings cannot be overstated. To be sure, the method of storage is not wholly aseptic; words often corrupt and modify the meanings they are supposed to keep intact, but liability to infection is a price paid by every living thing for the privilege of living.

A sign transfers a meaning

(c) When a meaning is detached and fixed by a sign, it is possible to use that meaning in a new context and situation. This transfer and reapplication is the key to all judgment and inference. It would little profit a man to recognize that a given particular cloud was the premonitor of a given particular rainstorm if his recognition ended there, for he would then have to learn over and over again, since the next cloud and the next rain are different events. No cumulative growth of intelligence would occur; experience might form habits of physical adaptation but it would not teach anything, for we should not be able to use a prior experience consciously to anticipate and regulate a further experience. To be able to use the past to judge and infer the new and unknown implies that, although the past thing has gone, its meaning abides in such a way as to be applicable in determining the character of the new. Speech forms are our great carriers: the easy-running vehicles by which meanings are transported from experiences that no longer concern us to those that are as yet dark and dubious.

Logical organization depends upon signs

II. Organization of Meanings. In emphasizing the importance of signs in relation to specific meanings, we have overlooked another aspect, equally valuable. Signs not only mark off specific or individual meanings, but they are also instruments of grouping meanings in relation to one another. Words are not only names or titles of single meanings; they also form sentences in which meanings are organized in relation to one another. When we say "That book is a dictionary," or "That blur of light in the heavens is Halley's comet," we express a logical connection—an act of classifying and defining that goes beyond the physical thing into the logical region of genera and species, things and attributes. Propositions, sentences, bear the same relation to judgments that distinct words, built up mainly by analyzing propositions in their various types, bear to meanings or conceptions; and just as words imply a sentence, so a sentence implies a larger whole of consecutive discourse into which it fits. As is often said, grammar expresses the unconscious logic of the popular mind. The chief intellectual classifications that constitute the working capital of thought have been built up for us by our mother tongue. Our very lack of explicit consciousness in using language that we are employing the intellectual systematizations of the race shows how thoroughly accustomed we have become to its logical distinctions and groupings.

§ 2. The Abuse of Linguistic Methods in Education

Teaching merely things, not educative

Taken literally, the maxim, "Teach things, not words," or "Teach things before words," would be the negation of education; it would reduce mental life to mere physical and sensible adjustments. Learning, in the proper sense, is not learning things, but the meanings of things, and this process involves the use of signs, or language in its generic sense. In like fashion, the warfare of some educational reformers against symbols, if pushed to extremes, involves the destruction of the intellectual life, since this lives, moves, and has its being in those processes of definition, abstraction, generalization, and classification that are made possible by symbols alone. Nevertheless, these contentions of educational reformers have been needed. The liability of a thing to abuse is in proportion to the value of its right use.

But words separated from things are not true signs

Symbols are themselves, as pointed out above, particular, physical, sensible existences, like any other things. They are symbols only by virtue of what they suggest and represent, i.e. meanings. (i) They stand for these meanings to any individual only when he has had experience of some situation to which these meanings are actually relevant. Words can detach and preserve a meaning only when the meaning has been first involved in our own direct intercourse with things. To attempt to give a meaning through a word alone without any dealings with a thing is to deprive the word of intelligible signification; against this attempt, a tendency only too prevalent in education, reformers have protested. Moreover, there is a tendency to assume that whenever there is a definite word or form of speech there is also a definite idea; while, as a matter of fact, adults and children alike are capable of using even precise verbal formulæ with only the vaguest and most confused sense of what they mean. Genuine ignorance is more profitable because likely to be accompanied by humility, curiosity, and open-mindedness; while ability to repeat catch-phrases, cant terms, familiar propositions, gives the conceit of learning and coats the mind with a varnish waterproof to new ideas.

Language tends to arrest personal inquiry and reflection

(ii) Again, although new combinations of words without the intervention of physical things may supply new ideas, there are limits to this possibility. Lazy inertness causes individuals to accept ideas that have currency about them without personal inquiry and testing. A man uses thought, perhaps, to find out what others believe, and then stops. The ideas of others as embodied in language become substitutes for one's own ideas. The use of linguistic studies and methods to halt the human mind on the level of the attainments of the past, to prevent new inquiry and discovery, to put the authority of tradition in place of the authority of natural facts and laws, to reduce the individual to a parasite living on the secondhand experience of others—these things have been the source of the reformers' protest against the preëminence assigned to language in schools.

Words as mere stimuli

Finally, words that originally stood for ideas come, with repeated use, to be mere counters; they become physical things to be manipulated according to certain rules, or reacted to by certain operations without consciousness of their meaning. Mr. Stout (who has called such terms "substitute signs") remarks that "algebraical and arithmetical signs are to a great extent used as mere substitute signs.... It is possible to use signs of this kind whenever fixed and definite rules of operation can be derived from the nature of the things symbolized, so as to be applied in manipulating the signs, without further reference to their signification. A word is an instrument for thinking about the meaning which it expresses; a substitute sign is a means of not thinking about the meaning which it symbolizes." The principle applies, however, to ordinary words, as well as to algebraic signs; they also enable us to use meanings so as to get results without thinking. In many respects, signs that are means of not thinking are of great advantage; standing for the familiar, they release attention for meanings that, being novel, require conscious interpretation. Nevertheless, the premium put in the schoolroom upon attainment of technical facility, upon skill in producing external results (ante, p. 51), often changes this advantage into a positive detriment. In manipulating symbols so as to recite well, to get and give correct answers, to follow prescribed formulæ of analysis, the pupil's attitude becomes mechanical, rather than thoughtful; verbal memorizing is substituted for inquiry into the meaning of things. This danger is perhaps the one uppermost in mind when verbal methods of education are attacked.

§ 3. The Use of Language in its Educational Bearings

Language stands in a twofold relation to the work of education. On the one hand, it is continually used in all studies as well as in all the social discipline of the school; on the other, it is a distinct object of study. We shall consider only the ordinary use of language, since its effects upon habits of thought are much deeper than those of conscious study.

Language not primarily intellectual in purpose

The common statement that "language is the expression of thought" conveys only a half-truth, and a half-truth that is likely to result in positive error. Language does express thought, but not primarily, nor, at first, even consciously. The primary motive for language is to influence (through the expression of desire, emotion, and thought) the activity of others; its secondary use is to enter into more intimate sociable relations with them; its employment as a conscious vehicle of thought and knowledge is a tertiary, and relatively late, formation. The contrast is well brought out by the statement of John Locke that words have a double use—"civil" and "philosophical." "By their civil use, I mean such a communication of thoughts and ideas by words as may serve for the upholding of common conversation and commerce about the ordinary affairs and conveniences of civil life.... By the philosophical use of words, I mean such a use of them as may serve to convey the precise notions of things, and to express in general propositions certain and undoubted truths."

Hence education has to transform it into an intellectual tool

This distinction of the practical and social from the intellectual use of language throws much light on the problem of the school in respect to speech. That problem is to direct pupils' oral and written speech, used primarily for practical and social ends, so that gradually it shall become a conscious tool of conveying knowledge and assisting thought. How without checking the spontaneous, natural motives—motives to which language owes its vitality, force, vividness, and variety—are we to modify speech habits so as to render them accurate and flexible intellectual instruments? It is comparatively easy to encourage the original spontaneous flow and not make language over into a servant of reflective thought; it is comparatively easy to check and almost destroy (so far as the schoolroom is concerned) native aim and interest, and to set up artificial and formal modes of expression in some isolated and technical matters. The difficulty lies in making over habits that have to do with "ordinary affairs and conveniences" into habits concerned with "precise notions." The successful accomplishing of the transformation requires (i) enlargement of the pupil's vocabulary; (ii) rendering its terms more precise and accurate, and (iii) formation of habits of consecutive discourse.

To enlarge vocabulary, the fund of concepts should be enlarged

(i) *Enlargement of vocabulary.* This takes place, of course, by wider intelligent contact with things and persons, and also vicariously, by gathering the meanings of words from the context in which they are heard or read. To grasp by either method a word in its meaning is to exercise intelligence, to perform an act of intelligent selection or analysis, and it is also to widen the fund of meanings or concepts readily available in further intellectual enterprises. It is usual to distinguish between one's active and one's passive vocabulary, the latter being composed of the words that are understood when they are heard or seen, the former of words that are used intelligently. The fact that the passive vocabulary is ordinarily much larger than the active indicates a certain amount of inert energy, of power not freely controlled by an individual. Failure to use meanings that are nevertheless understood reveals dependence upon external stimulus, and lack of intellectual initiative. This mental laziness is to some extent an artificial product of education. Small children usually attempt to put to use every new word they get hold of, but when they learn to read they are introduced to a large variety of terms that there is no ordinary opportunity to use. The result is a kind of mental suppression, if not smothering. Moreover, the meaning of words not actively used in building up and conveying ideas is never quite clear-cut or complete.

Looseness of thinking accompanies a limited vocabulary

While a limited vocabulary may be due to a limited range of experience, to a sphere of contact with persons and things so narrow as not to suggest or require a full store of words, it is also due to carelessness and vagueness. A happy-go-lucky frame of mind makes the individual averse to clear discriminations, either in perception or in his own speech. Words are used loosely in an indeterminate kind of reference to things, and the mind approaches a condition where practically everything is just a thing-um-bob or a what-do-you-call-it. Paucity of vocabulary on the part of those with whom the child associates, triviality and meagerness in the child's reading matter (as frequently even in his school readers and text-books), tend to shut down the area of mental vision.

Command of language involves command of things

We must note also the great difference between flow of words and command of language. Volubility is not necessarily a sign of a large vocabulary; much talking or even ready speech is quite compatible with moving round and round in a circle of moderate radius. Most schoolrooms suffer from a lack of materials and appliances save perhaps books—and even these are "written down" to the supposed capacity, or incapacity, of children. Occasion and demand for an enriched vocabulary are accordingly restricted. The vocabulary of things studied in the schoolroom is very largely isolated; it does not link itself organically to the range of the ideas and words that are in vogue outside the school. Hence the enlargement that takes place is often nominal, adding to the inert, rather than to the active, fund of meanings and terms.

(ii) *Accuracy of vocabulary*. One way in which the fund of words and concepts is increased is by discovering and naming shades of meaning—that is to say, by making the vocabulary more precise. Increase in definiteness is as important relatively as is the enlargement of the capital stock absolutely.

The general as the vague and as the distinctly generic

The first meanings of terms, since they are due to superficial acquaintance with things, are general in the sense of being vague. The little child calls all men papa; acquainted with a dog, he may call the first horse he sees a big dog. Differences of quantity and intensity are noted, but the fundamental meaning is so vague that it covers things that are far apart. To many persons trees are just trees, being discriminated only into deciduous trees and evergreens, with perhaps recognition of one or two kinds of each. Such vagueness tends to persist and to become a barrier to the advance of thinking. Terms that are miscellaneous in scope are clumsy tools at best; in addition they are frequently treacherous, for their ambiguous reference causes us to confuse things that should be distinguished.

Twofold growth of words in sense or signification

The growth of precise terms out of original vagueness takes place normally in two directions: toward words that stand for relationships and words that stand for highly individualized traits; the first being associated with abstract, the second with concrete, thinking. Some Australian tribes are said to have no words for animal or for plant, while they have specific names for every variety of plant and animal in their neighborhoods.

This minuteness of vocabulary represents progress toward definiteness, but in a one-sided way. Specific properties are distinguished, but not relationships. On the other hand, students of philosophy and of the general aspects of natural and social science are apt to acquire a store of terms that signify relations without balancing them up with terms that designate specific individuals and traits. The ordinary use of such terms as causation, law, society, individual, capital, illustrates this tendency.

Words alter their meanings so as to change their logical functions

In the history of language we find both aspects of the growth of vocabulary illustrated by changes in the sense of words: some words originally wide in their application are narrowed to denote shades of meaning; others originally specific are widened to express relationships. The term vernacular, now meaning mother speech, has been generalized from the word *verna*, meaning a slave born in the master's household. Publication has evolved its meaning of communication by means of print, through restricting an earlier meaning of any kind of communication—although the wider meaning is retained in legal procedure, as publishing a libel. The sense of the word average has been generalized from a use connected with dividing loss by shipwreck proportionately among various sharers in an enterprise.

Similar changes occur in the vocabulary of every student

These historical changes assist the educator to appreciate the changes that occur with individuals together with advance in intellectual resources. In studying geometry, a pupil must learn both to narrow and to extend the meanings of such familiar words as line, surface, angle, square, circle; to narrow them to the precise meanings involved in demonstrations; to extend them to cover generic relations not expressed in ordinary usage. Qualities of color and size must be excluded; relations of direction, of variation in direction, of limit, must be definitely seized. A like transformation occurs, of course, in every subject of study. Just at this point lies the danger, alluded to above, of simply overlaying common meanings with new and isolated meanings instead of effecting a genuine working-over of popular and practical meanings into adequate logical tools.

The value of technical terms

Terms used with intentional exactness so as to express a meaning, the whole meaning, and only the meaning, are called technical. For educational purposes, a technical term indicates something relative, not absolute; for a term is technical not because of its verbal form or its unusualness, but because it is employed to fix a meaning precisely. Ordinary words get a technical quality when used intentionally for this end. Whenever thought becomes more accurate, a (relatively) technical vocabulary grows up. Teachers are apt to oscillate between extremes in regard to technical terms. On the one hand, these are multiplied in every direction, seemingly on the assumption that learning a new piece of terminology, accompanied by verbal description or definition, is equivalent to grasping a new idea. When it is seen how largely the net outcome is the accumulation of an isolated set of words, a jargon or scholastic cant, and to what extent the natural power of judgment is clogged by this accumulation, there is a reaction to the opposite extreme. Technical terms are banished: "name words" exist but not nouns; "action words" but not verbs; pupils may "take away," but not subtract; they may tell what four fives are, but not what four times five are, and so on. A sound instinct underlies this reaction—aversion to words that give the pretense, but not the reality, of meaning. Yet the fundamental difficulty is not with the word, but with the idea. If the idea is not grasped, nothing is gained by using a more familiar word; if the idea is perceived, the use of the term that exactly names it may assist in fixing the idea. Terms denoting highly exact meanings should be introduced only sparingly, that is, a few at a time; they should be led up to gradually, and great pains should be taken to secure the circumstances that render precision of meaning significant.

Importance of consecutive discourse

(iii) *Consecutive discourse*. As we saw, language connects and organizes meanings as well as selects and fixes them. As every meaning is set in the context of some situation, so every word in concrete use belongs to some sentence (it may itself represent a condensed sentence), and the sentence, in turn, belongs to some larger story, description, or reasoning process. It is unnecessary to repeat what has been said about the importance of continuity and ordering of meanings. We may, however, note some ways in which school practices tend to interrupt consecutiveness of language and thereby interfere harmfully with systematic reflection. (a) Teachers have a habit of monopolizing continued discourse. Many, if not most, instructors would be surprised if informed at the end of the day of the amount of time they have talked as compared with any pupil. Children's conversation is often confined to answering questions in brief phrases, or in single disconnected sentences. Expatiation and explanation are reserved for the teacher, who often admits any hint at an answer on the part of the pupil, and then amplifies what he supposes the child must have meant. The habits of sporadic and fragmentary discourse thus promoted have inevitably a disintegrating intellectual influence.

Too minute questioning

(b) Assignment of too short lessons when accompanied (as it usually is in order to pass the time of the recitation period) by minute "analytic" questioning has the same effect. This evil is usually at its height in such subjects as history and literature, where not infrequently the material is so minutely subdivided as to break up the unity of meaning belonging to a given portion of the matter, to destroy perspective, and in effect to reduce the whole topic to an accumulation of disconnected details all upon the same level. More often than the teacher is aware, his mind carries and supplies the background of unity of meaning against which pupils project isolated scraps.

Making avoidance of error the aim

(c) Insistence upon avoiding error instead of attaining power tends also to interruption of continuous discourse and thought. Children who begin with something to say and with intellectual eagerness to say it are sometimes made so conscious of minor errors in substance and form that the energy that should go into constructive thinking is diverted into anxiety not to make mistakes, and even, in extreme cases, into passive quiescence as the best method of minimizing error. This tendency is especially marked in connection with the writing of compositions, essays, and themes. It has even been gravely recommended that little children should always write on trivial subjects and in short sentences because in that way they are less likely to make mistakes, while the teaching of writing to high school and college students occasionally reduces itself to a technique for detecting and designating mistakes. The resulting self-consciousness and constraint are only part of the evil that comes from a negative ideal.

Chapter Fourteen

Observation and Information In The Training of Mind

No thinking without acquaintance with facts

Thinking is an ordering of subject-matter with reference to discovering what it signifies or indicates. Thinking no more exists apart from this arranging of subject-matter than digestion occurs apart from the assimilating of food. The way in which the subject-matter is furnished marks, therefore, a fundamental point. If the subject-matter is provided in too scanty or too profuse fashion, if it comes in disordered array or in isolated scraps, the effect upon habits of thought is detrimental. If personal observation and communication of information by others (whether in books or speech) are rightly conducted, half the logical battle is won, for they are the channels of obtaining subject-matter.

§ 1. The Nature and Value of Observation

Fallacy of making "facts" an end in themselves

The protest, mentioned in the last chapter, of educational reformers against the exaggerated and false use of language, insisted upon personal and direct observation as the proper alternative course. The reformers felt that the current emphasis upon the linguistic factor eliminated all opportunity for first-hand acquaintance with real things; hence they appealed to sense-perception to fill the gap. It is not surprising that this enthusiastic zeal failed frequently to ask how and why observation is educative, and hence fell into the error of making observation an end in itself and was satisfied with any kind of material under any kind of conditions. Such isolation of observation is still manifested in the statement that this faculty develops first, then that of memory and imagination, and finally the faculty of thought. From this point of view, observation is regarded as furnishing crude masses of raw material, to which, later on, reflective processes may be applied. Our previous pages should have made obvious the fallacy of this point of view by bringing out the fact that simple concrete thinking attends all our intercourse with things which is not on a purely physical level.

The sympathetic motive in extending acquaintance

I. All persons have a natural desire—akin to curiosity—for a widening of their range of acquaintance with persons and things. The sign in art galleries that for bids the carrying of canes and umbrellas is obvious testimony to the fact that simply to see is not enough for many people; there is a feeling of lack of acquaintance until some direct contact is made. This demand for fuller and closer knowledge is quite different from any conscious interest in observation for its own sake. Desire for expansion, for "self-realization," is its motive. The interest is sympathetic, socially and æsthetically sympathetic, rather than cognitive. While the interest is especially keen in children (because their actual experience is so small and their possible experience so large), it still characterizes adults when routine has not blunted its edge. This sympathetic interest provides the medium for carrying and binding together what would otherwise be a multitude of items, diverse, disconnected, and of no intellectual use. These systems are indeed social and æsthetic rather than consciously intellectual; but they provide the natural medium for more conscious intellectual explorations. Some educators have recommended that nature study in the elementary schools be conducted with a love of nature and a cultivation of æsthetic appreciation in view rather than in a purely analytic spirit. Others have urged making much of the care of animals and plants. Both of these important recommendations have grown out of experience, not out of theory, but they afford excellent exemplifications of the theoretic point just made.

Analytic inspection for the sake of doing

Direct and indirect sense training

II. In normal development, specific analytic observations are originally connected almost exclusively with the imperative need for noting means and ends in carrying on activities. When one is doing something, one is compelled, if the work is to succeed (unless it is purely routine), to use eyes, ears, and sense of touch as guides to action. Without a constant and alert exercise of the senses, not even plays and games can go on; in any form of work, materials, obstacles, appliances, failures, and successes, must be intently watched. Sense-perception does not occur for its own sake or for purposes of training, but because it is an indispensable factor of success in doing what one is interested in doing. Although not designed for sense-training, this method effects sense-training in the most economical and thoroughgoing way. Various schemes have been designed by teachers for cultivating sharp and prompt observation of forms, as by writing words—even in an unknown language—making arrangements of figures and geometrical forms, and having pupils reproduce them after a momentary glance. Children often attain great skill in quick seeing and full reproducing of even complicated meaningless combinations. But such methods of training—however valuable as occasional games and diversions—compare very unfavorably with the training of eye and hand that comes as an incident of work with tools in wood or metals, or of gardening, cooking, or the care of animals. Training by isolated exercises leaves no deposit, leads nowhere; and even the technical skill acquired has little radiating power, or transferable value. Criticisms made upon the training of observation on the ground that many persons cannot correctly reproduce the forms and arrangement of the figures on the face of their watches misses the point because persons do not look at a watch to find out whether four o'clock is indicated by IIII or by IV, but to find out what time it is, and, if observation decides this matter, noting other details is irrelevant and a waste of time. In the training of observation the question of end and motive is all-important.

Scientific observations are linked to problems

"Object-lessons" rarely supply problems

III. The further, more intellectual or scientific, development of observation follows the line of the growth of practical into theoretical reflection already traced (ante, Chapter Ten). As problems emerge and are dwelt upon, observation is directed less to the facts that bear upon a practical aim and more upon what bears upon a problem as such. What makes observations in schools often intellectually ineffective is (more than anything else) that they are carried on independently of a sense of a problem that they serve to define or help to solve. The evil of this isolation is seen through the entire educational system, from the kindergarten, through the elementary and high schools, to the college. Almost everywhere may be found, at some time, recourse to observations as if they were of complete and final value in themselves, instead of the means of getting material that bears upon some difficulty and its solution. In the kindergarten are heaped up observations regarding geometrical forms, lines, surfaces, cubes, colors, and so on. In the elementary school, under the name of "object-lessons," the form and properties of objects,—apple, orange, chalk,—selected almost at random, are minutely noted, while under the name of "nature study" similar observations are directed upon leaves, stones, insects, selected in almost equally arbitrary fashion. In high school and college, laboratory and microscopic observations are carried on as if the accumulation of observed facts and the acquisition of skill in manipulation were educational ends in themselves.

Compare with these methods of isolated observations the statement of Jevons that observation as conducted by scientific men is effective "only when excited and guided by hope of verifying a theory"; and again, "the number of things which can be observed and experimented upon are infinite, and if we merely set to work to record facts without any distinct purpose, our records will have no value." Strictly speaking, the first statement of Jevons is too narrow. Scientific men institute observations not merely to test an idea (or suggested explanatory meaning), but also to locate the nature of a problem and thereby guide the formation of a hypothesis. But the principle of his remark, namely, that scientific men never make the accumulation of observations an end in itself, but always a means to a general intellectual conclusion, is absolutely sound. Until the force of this principle is adequately recognized in education, observation will be largely a matter of uninteresting dead work or of acquiring forms of technical skill that are not available as intellectual resources.

§ 2. Methods and Materials of Observation in the Schools

The best methods in use in our schools furnish many suggestions for giving observation its right place in mental training.

Observation should involve discovery

I. They rest upon the sound assumption that observation is an active process. Observation is exploration, inquiry for the sake of discovering something previously hidden and unknown, this something being needed in order to reach some end, practical or theoretical. Observation is to be discriminated from recognition, or perception of what is familiar. The identification of something already understood is, indeed, an indispensable function of further investigation; but it is relatively automatic and passive, while observation proper is searching and deliberate. Recognition refers to the already mastered; observation is concerned with mastering the unknown. The common notions that perception is like writing on a blank piece of paper, or like impressing an image on the mind as a seal is imprinted on wax or as a picture is formed on a photographic plate (notions that have played a disastrous rôle in educational methods), arise from a failure to distinguish between automatic recognition and the searching attitude of genuine observation.

And suspense during an unfolding change

II. Much assistance in the selection of appropriate material for observation may be derived from considering the eagerness and closeness of observation that attend the following of a story or drama. Alertness of observation is at its height wherever there is "plot interest." Why? Because of the balanced combination of the old and the new, of the familiar and the unexpected. We hang on the lips of the story-teller because of the element of mental suspense. Alternatives are suggested, but are left ambiguous, so that our whole being questions: What befell next? Which way did things turn out? Contrast the ease and fullness with which a child notes all the salient traits of a story, with the labor and inadequacy of his observation of some dead and static thing where nothing raises a question or suggests alternative outcomes.

This "plot interest" manifested in activity

When an individual is engaged in doing or making something (the activity not being of such a mechanical and habitual character that its outcome is assured), there is an analogous situation. Something is going to come of what is present to the sense, but just what is doubtful. The plot is unfolding toward success or failure, but just when or how is uncertain. Hence the keen and tense observation of conditions and results that attends constructive manual operations. Where the subject-matter is of a more impersonal sort, the same principle of movement toward a dénouement may apply. It is a commonplace that what is moving attracts notice when that which is at rest escapes it. Yet too often it would almost seem as if pains had been taken to deprive the material of school observations of all life and dramatic quality, to reduce it to a dead and inert form. Mere change is not enough, however. Vicissitude, alteration, motion, excite observation; but if they merely excite it, there is no thought. The changes must (like the incidents of a well-arranged story or plot) take place in a certain cumulative order; each successive change must at once remind us of its predecessor and arouse interest in its successor if observations of change are to be logically fruitful.

And in cycles of growth

Living beings, plants, and animals, fulfill the twofold requirement to an extraordinary degree. Where there is growth, there is motion, change, process; and there is also arrangement of the changes in a cycle. The first arouses, the second organizes, observation. Much of the extraordinary interest that children take in planting seeds and watching the stages of their growth is due to the fact that a drama is enacting before their eyes; there is something doing, each step of which is important in the destiny of the plant. The great practical improvements that have occurred of late years in the teaching of botany and zoölogy will be found, upon inspection, to involve treating plants and animals as beings that act, that do something, instead of as mere inert specimens having static properties to be inventoried, named, and registered. Treated in the latter fashion, observation is inevitably reduced to the falsely "analytic"—to mere dissection and enumeration.

Observation of structure grows out of noting function

There is, of course, a place, and an important place, for observation of the mere static qualities of objects. When, however, the primary interest is in function, in what the object does, there is a motive for more minute analytic study, for the observation of structure. Interest in noting an activity passes insensibly into noting how the activity is carried on; the interest in what is accomplished passes over into an interest in the organs of its accomplishing. But when the beginning is made with the morphological, the anatomical, the noting of peculiarities of form, size, color, and distribution of parts, the material is so cut off from significance as to be dead and dull. It is as natural for children to look intently for the stomata of a plant after they have become interested in its function of breathing, as it is repulsive to attend minutely to them when they are considered as isolated peculiarities of structure.

Scientific observation

III. As the center of interest of observations becomes less personal, less a matter of means for effecting one's own ends, and less æsthetic, less a matter of contribution of parts to a total emotional effect, observation becomes more consciously intellectual in quality. Pupils learn to observe for the sake (i) of finding out what sort of perplexity confronts them; (ii) of inferring hypothetical explanations for the puzzling features that observation reveals; and (iii) of testing the ideas thus suggested.

Should be extensive and intensive

In short, observation becomes scientific in nature. Of such observations it may be said that they should follow a rhythm between the extensive and the intensive. Problems become definite, and suggested explanations significant by a certain alternation between a wide and somewhat loose soaking in of relevant facts and a minutely accurate study of a few selected facts. The wider, less exact observation is necessary to give the student a feeling for the reality of the field of inquiry, a sense of its bearings and possibilities, and to store his mind with materials that imagination may transform into suggestions. The intensive study is necessary for limiting the problem, and for securing the conditions of experimental testing. As the latter by itself is too specialized and technical to arouse intellectual growth, the former by itself is too superficial and scattering for control of intellectual development. In the sciences of life, field study, excursions, acquaintance with living things in their natural habitats, may alternate with microscopic and laboratory observation. In the physical sciences, phenomena of light, of heat, of electricity, of moisture, of gravity, in their broad setting in nature—their physiographic setting—should prepare for an exact study of selected facts under conditions of laboratory control. In this way, the student gets the benefit of technical scientific methods of discovery and testing, while he retains his sense of the identity of the laboratory modes of energy with large out-of-door realities, thereby avoiding the impression (that so often accrues) that the facts studied are peculiar to the laboratory.

§ 3. Communication of Information

Importance of hearsay acquaintance

When all is said and done the field of fact open to any one observer by himself is narrow. Into every one of our beliefs, even those that we have worked out under the conditions of utmost personal, first-hand acquaintance, much has insensibly entered from what we have heard or read of the observations and conclusions of others. In spite of the great extension of direct observation in our schools, the vast bulk of educational subject-matter is derived from other sources—from text-book, lecture, and viva-voce interchange. No educational question is of greater import than how to get the most logical good out of learning through transmission from others.

Logically, this ranks only as evidence or testimony

Doubtless the chief meaning associated with the word instruction is this conveying and instilling of the results of the observations and inferences of others. Doubtless the undue prominence in education of the ideal of amassing information (ante, p. 52) has its source in the prominence of the learning of other persons. The problem then is how to convert it into an intellectual asset. In logical terms, the material supplied from the experience of others is testimony: that is to say, evidence submitted by others to be employed by one's own judgment in reaching a conclusion. How shall we treat the subject-matter supplied by text-book and teacher so that it shall rank as material for reflective inquiry, not as ready-made intellectual pabulum to be accepted and swallowed just as supplied by the store?

Communication by others should not encroach on observation,

In reply to this question, we may say (i) that the communication of material should be needed. That is to say, it should be such as cannot readily be attained by personal observation. For teacher or book to cram pupils with facts which, with little more trouble, they could discover by direct inquiry is to violate their intellectual integrity by cultivating mental servility. This does not mean that the material supplied through communication of others should be meager or scanty. With the utmost range of the senses, the world of nature and history stretches out almost infinitely beyond. But the fields within which direct observation is feasible should be carefully chosen and sacredly protected.

Should not be dogmatic in tone

(ii) Material should be supplied by way of stimulus, not with dogmatic finality and rigidity. When pupils get the notion that any field of study has been definitely surveyed, that knowledge about it is exhaustive and final, they may continue docile pupils, but they cease to be students. All thinking whatsoever—so be it is thinking—contains a phase of originality. This originality does not imply that the student's conclusion varies from the conclusions of others, much less that it is a radically novel conclusion. His originality is not incompatible with large use of materials and suggestions contributed by others. Originality means personal interest in the question, personal initiative in turning over the suggestions furnished by others, and sincerity in following them out to a tested conclusion. Literally, the phrase "Think for yourself" is tautological; any thinking is thinking for one's self.

Should have relation to a personal problem

(iii) The material furnished by way of information should be relevant to a question that is vital in the student's own experience. What has been said about the evil of observations that begin and end in themselves may be transferred without change to communicated learning. Instruction in subject-matter that does not fit into any problem already stirring in the student's own experience, or that is not presented in such a way as to arouse a problem, is worse than useless for intellectual purposes. In that it fails to enter into any process of reflection, it is useless; in that it remains in the mind as so much lumber and débris, it is a barrier, an obstruction in the way of effective thinking when a problem arises.

And to prior systems of experience

Another way of stating the same principle is that material furnished by communication must be such as to enter into some existing system or organization of experience. All students of psychology are familiar with the principle of apperception—that we assimilate new material with what we have digested and retained from prior experiences. Now the "apperceptive basis" of material furnished by teacher and text-book should be found, as far as possible, in what the learner has derived from more direct forms of his own experience. There is a tendency to connect material of the schoolroom simply with the material of prior school lessons, instead of linking it to what the pupil has acquired in his out-of-school experience. The teacher says, "Do you not remember what we learned from the book last week?"—instead of saying, "Do you not recall such and such a thing that you have seen or heard?" As a result, there are built up detached and independent systems of school knowledge that inertly overlay the ordinary systems of experience instead of reacting to enlarge and refine them. Pupils are taught to live in two separate worlds, one the world of out-of-school experience, the other the world of books and lessons.

Chapter Fifteen

The Recitation and the Training of Thought

Importance of the recitation

In the recitation the teacher comes into his closest contact with the pupil. In the recitation focus the possibilities of guiding children's activities, influencing their language habits, and directing their observations. In discussing the significance of the recitation as an instrumentality of education, we are accordingly bringing to a head the points considered in the last three chapters, rather than introducing a new topic. The method in which the recitation is carried on is a crucial test of a teacher's skill in diagnosing the intellectual state of his pupils and in supplying the conditions that will arouse serviceable mental responses: in short, of his art as a teacher.

Re-citing versus reflecting

The use of the word recitation to designate the period of most intimate intellectual contact of teacher with pupil and pupil with pupil is a fateful fact. To re-cite is to cite again, to repeat, to tell over and over. If we were to call this period reiteration, the designation would hardly bring out more clearly than does the word recitation, the complete domination of instruction by rehearsing of secondhand information, by memorizing for the sake of producing correct replies at the proper time. Everything that is said in this chapter is insignificant in comparison with the primary truth that the recitation is a place and time for stimulating and directing reflection, and that reproducing memorized matter is only an incident—even though an indispensable incident—in the process of cultivating a thoughtful attitude.

§ 1. The Formal Steps of Instruction

Herbart's analysis of method of teaching

But few attempts have been made to formulate a method, resting on general principles, of conducting a recitation. One of these is of great importance and has probably had more and better influence upon the "hearing of lessons" than all others put together; namely, the analysis by Herbart of a recitation into five successive steps. The steps are commonly known as "the formal steps of instruction." The underlying notion is that no matter how subjects vary in scope and detail there is one and only one best way of mastering them, since there is a single "general method" uniformly followed by the mind in effective attack upon any subject. Whether it be a first-grade child mastering the rudiments of number, a grammar-school pupil studying history, or a college student dealing with philology, in each case the first step is preparation, the second presentation, followed in turn by comparison and generalization, ending in the application of the generalizations to specific and new instances.

Illustration of method

By preparation is meant asking questions to remind pupils of familiar experiences of their own that will be useful in acquiring the new topic. What one already knows supplies the means with which one apprehends the unknown. Hence the process of learning the new will be made easier if related ideas in the pupil's mind are aroused to activity—are brought to the foreground of consciousness. When pupils take up the study of rivers, they are first questioned about streams or brooks with which they are already acquainted; if they have never seen any, they may be asked about water running in gutters. Somehow "apperceptive masses" are stirred that will assist in getting hold of the new subject. The step of preparation ends with statement of the aim of the lesson. Old knowledge having been made active, new material is then "presented" to the pupils. Pictures and relief models of rivers are shown; vivid oral descriptions are given; if possible, the children are taken to see an actual river. These two steps terminate the acquisition of particular facts.

The next two steps are directed toward getting a general principle or conception. The local river is compared with, perhaps, the Amazon, the St. Lawrence, the Rhine; by this comparison accidental and unessential features are eliminated and the river concept is formed: the elements involved in the river-meaning are gathered together and formulated. This done, the resulting principle is fixed in mind and is clarified by being applied to other streams, say to the Thames, the Po, the Connecticut.

Comparison with our prior analysis of reflection

If we compare this account of the methods of instruction with our own analysis of a complete operation of thinking, we are struck by obvious resemblances. In our statement (compare Chapter Six) the "steps" are the occurrence of a problem or a puzzling phenomenon; then observation, inspection of facts, to locate and clear up the problem; then the formation of a hypothesis or the suggestion of a possible solution together with its elaboration by reasoning; then the testing of the elaborated idea by using it as a guide to new observations and experimentations. In each account, there is the sequence of (i) specific facts and events, (ii) ideas and reasonings, and (iii) application of their result to specific facts. In each case, the movement is inductive-deductive. We are struck also by one difference: the Herbartian method makes no reference to a difficulty, a discrepancy requiring explanation, as the origin and stimulus of the whole process. As a consequence, it often seems as if the Herbartian method deals with thought simply as an incident in the process of acquiring information, instead of treating the latter as an incident in the process of developing thought.

The formal steps concern the teacher's preparation rather than the recitation itself

Before following up this comparison in more detail, we may raise the question whether the recitation should, in any case, follow a uniform prescribed series of steps—even if it be admitted that this series expresses the normal logical order. In reply, it may be said that just because the order is logical, it represents the survey of subject-matter made by one who already understands it, not the path of progress followed by a mind that is learning. The former may describe a uniform straight-way course, the latter must be a series of tacks, of zigzag movements back and forth. In short, the formal steps indicate the points that should be covered by the teacher in preparing to conduct a recitation, but should not prescribe the actual course of teaching.

The teacher's problem

Lack of any preparation on the part of a teacher leads, of course, to a random, haphazard recitation, its success depending on the inspiration of the moment, which may or may not come. Preparation in simply the subject-matter conduces to a rigid order, the teacher examining pupils on their exact knowledge of their text. But the teacher's problem—as a teacher—does not reside in mastering a subject-matter, but in adjusting a subject-matter to the nurture of thought. Now the formal steps indicate excellently well the questions a teacher should ask in working out the problem of teaching a topic. What preparation have my pupils for attacking this subject? What familiar experiences of theirs are available? What have they already learned that will come to their assistance? How shall I present the matter so as to fit economically and effectively into their present equipment? What pictures shall I show? To what objects shall I call their attention? What incidents shall I relate? What comparisons shall I lead them to draw, what similarities to recognize? What is the general principle toward which the whole discussion should point as its conclusion? By what applications shall I try to fix, to clear up, and to make real their grasp of this general principle? What activities of their own may bring it home to them as a genuinely significant principle?

Only flexibility of procedure gives a recitation vitality

Any step may come first

No teacher can fail to teach better if he has considered such questions somewhat systematically. But the more the teacher has reflected upon pupils' probable intellectual response to a topic from the various standpoints indicated by the five formal steps, the more he will be prepared to conduct the recitation in a flexible and free way, and yet not let the subject go to pieces and the pupils' attention drift in all directions; the less necessary will he find it, in order to preserve a semblance of intellectual order, to follow some one uniform scheme. He will be ready to take advantage of any sign of vital response that shows itself from any direction. One pupil may already have some inkling—probably erroneous—of a general principle. Application may then come at the very beginning in order to show that the principle will not work, and thereby induce search for new facts and a new generalization. Or the abrupt presentation of some fact or object may so stimulate the minds of pupils as to render quite superfluous any preliminary preparation. If pupils' minds are at work at all, it is quite impossible that they should wait until the teacher has conscientiously taken them through the steps of preparation, presentation, and comparison before they form at least a working hypothesis or generalization. Moreover, unless comparison of the familiar and the unfamiliar is introduced at the beginning, both preparation and presentation will be aimless and without logical motive, isolated, and in so far meaningless. The student's mind cannot be prepared at large, but only for something in particular, and presentation is usually the best way of evoking associations. The emphasis may fall now on the familiar concept that will help grasp the new, now on the new facts that frame the problem; but in either case it is comparison and contrast with the other term of the pair which gives either its force. In short, to transfer the logical steps from the points that the teacher needs to consider to uniform successive steps in the conduct of a recitation, is to impose the logical review of a mind that already understands the subject, upon the mind that is struggling to comprehend it, and thereby to obstruct the logic of the student's own mind.

§ 2. The Factors in the Recitation

Bearing in mind that the formal steps represent intertwined factors of a student's progress and not mileposts on a beaten highway, we may consider each by itself. In so doing, it will be convenient to follow the example of many of the Herbartians and reduce the steps to three: first, the apprehension of specific or particular facts; second, rational generalization; third, application and verification.

Preparation is getting the sense of a problem

I. The processes having to do with particular facts are preparation and presentation. The best, indeed the only preparation is arousal to a perception of something that needs explanation, something unexpected, puzzling, peculiar. When the feeling of a genuine perplexity lays hold of any mind (no matter how the feeling arises), that mind is alert and inquiring, because stimulated from within. The shock, the bite, of a question will force the mind to go wherever it is capable of going, better than will the most ingenious pedagogical devices unaccompanied by this mental ardor. It is the sense of a problem that forces the mind to a survey and recall of the past to discover what the question means and how it may be dealt with.

Pitfalls in preparation

The teacher in his more deliberate attempts to call into play the familiar elements in a student's experience, must guard against certain dangers. (i) The step of preparation must not be too long continued or too exhaustive, or it defeats its own end. The pupil loses interest and is bored, when a plunge in medias res might have braced him to his work. The preparation part of the recitation period of some conscientious teachers reminds one of the boy who takes so long a run in order to gain headway for a jump that when he reaches the line, he is too tired to jump far. (ii) The organs by which we apprehend new material are our habits. To insist too minutely upon turning over habitual dispositions into conscious ideas is to interfere with their best workings. Some factors of familiar experience must indeed be brought to conscious recognition, just as transplanting is necessary for the best growth of some plants. But it is fatal to be forever digging up either experiences or plants to see how they are getting along. Constraint, self-consciousness, embarrassment, are the consequence of too much conscious refurbishing of familiar experiences.

Statement of aim of lesson

Strict Herbartians generally lay it down that statement—by the teacher—of the aim of a lesson is an indispensable part of preparation. This preliminary statement of the aim of the lesson hardly seems more intellectual in character, however, than tapping a bell or giving any other signal for attention and transfer of thoughts from diverting subjects. To the teacher the statement of an end is significant, because he has already been at the end; from a pupil's standpoint the statement of what he is going to learn is something of an Irish bull. If the statement of the aim is taken too seriously by the instructor, as meaning more than a signal to attention, its probable result is forestalling the pupil's own reaction, relieving him of the responsibility of developing a problem and thus arresting his mental initiative.

How much the teacher should tell or show

It is unnecessary to discuss at length presentation as a factor in the recitation, because our last chapter covered the topic under the captions of observation and communication. The function of presentation is to supply materials that force home the nature of a problem and furnish suggestions for dealing with it. The practical problem of the teacher is to preserve a balance between so little showing and telling as to fail to stimulate reflection and so much as to choke thought. Provided the student is genuinely engaged upon a topic, and provided the teacher is willing to give the student a good deal of leeway as to what he assimilates and retains (not requiring rigidly that everything be grasped or reproduced), there is comparatively little danger that one who is himself enthusiastic will communicate too much concerning a topic.

The pupil's responsibility for making out a reasonable case

II. The distinctively rational phase of reflective inquiry consists, as we have already seen, in the elaboration of an idea, or working hypothesis, through conjoint comparison and contrast, terminating in definition or formulation. (i) So far as the recitation is concerned, the primary requirement is that the student be held responsible for working out mentally every suggested principle so as to show what he means by it, how it bears upon the facts at hand, and how the facts bear upon it. Unless the pupil is made responsible for developing on his own account the reasonableness of the guess he puts forth, the recitation counts for practically nothing in the training of reasoning power. A clever teacher easily acquires great skill in dropping out the inept and senseless contributions of pupils, and in selecting and emphasizing those in line with the result he wishes to reach. But this method (sometimes called "suggestive questioning") relieves the pupils of intellectual responsibility, save for acrobatic agility in following the teacher's lead.

The necessity for mental leisure

(ii) The working over of a vague and more or less casual idea into coherent and definite form is impossible without a pause, without freedom from distraction. We say "Stop and think"; well, all reflection involves, at some point, stopping external observations and reactions so that an idea may mature. Meditation, withdrawal or abstraction from clamorous assailants of the senses and from demands for overt action, is as necessary at the reasoning stage, as are observation and experiment at other periods. The metaphors of digestion and assimilation, that so readily occur to mind in connection with rational elaboration, are highly instructive. A silent, uninterrupted working-over of considerations by comparing and weighing alternative suggestions, is indispensable for the development of coherent and compact conclusions. Reasoning is no more akin to disputing or arguing, or to the abrupt seizing and dropping of suggestions, than digestion is to a noisy champing of the jaws. The teacher must secure opportunity for leisurely mental digestion.

A typical central object necessary

(iii) In the process of comparison, the teacher must avert the distraction that ensues from putting before the mind a number of facts on the same level of importance. Since attention is selective, some one object normally claims thought and furnishes the center of departure and reference. This fact is fatal to the success of the pedagogical methods that endeavor to conduct comparison on the basis of putting before the mind a row of objects of equal importance. In comparing, the mind does not naturally begin with objects a, b, c, d, and try to find the respect in which they agree. It begins with a single object or situation more or less vague and inchoate in meaning, and makes excursions to other objects in order to render understanding of the central object consistent and clear. The mere multiplication of objects of comparison is adverse to successful reasoning. Each fact brought within the field of comparison should clear up some obscure feature or extend some fragmentary trait of the primary object.

Importance of types

In short, pains should be taken to see that the object on which thought centers is typical: material being typical when, although individual or specific, it is such as readily and fruitfully suggests the principles of an entire class of facts. No sane person begins to think about rivers wholesale or at large. He begins with the one river that has presented some puzzling trait. Then he studies other rivers to get light upon the baffling features of this one, and at the same time he employs the characteristic traits of his original object to reduce to order the multifarious details that appear in connection with other rivers. This working back and forth preserves unity of meaning, while protecting it from monotony and narrowness. Contrast, unlikeness, throws significant features into relief, and these become instruments for binding together into an organized or coherent meaning dissimilar characters. The mind is defended against the deadening influence of many isolated particulars and also against the barrenness of a merely formal principle. Particular cases and properties supply emphasis and concreteness; general principles convert the particulars into a single system.

All insight into meaning effects generalization

(iv) Hence generalization is not a separate and single act; it is rather a constant tendency and function of the entire discussion or recitation. Every step forward toward an idea that comprehends, that explains, that unites what was isolated and therefore puzzling, generalizes. The little child generalizes as truly as the adolescent or adult, even though he does not arrive at the same generalities. If he is studying a river basin, his knowledge is generalized in so far as the various details that he apprehends are found to be the effects of a single force, as that of water pushing downward from gravity, or are seen to be successive stages of a single history of formation. Even if there were acquaintance with only one river, knowledge of it under such conditions would be generalized knowledge.

Insight into meaning requires formulation

The factor of formulation, of conscious stating, involved in generalization, should also be a constant function, not a single formal act. Definition means essentially the growth of a meaning out of vagueness into definiteness. Such final verbal definition as takes place should be only the culmination of a steady growth in distinctness. In the reaction against ready-made verbal definitions and rules, the pendulum should never swing to the opposite extreme, that of neglecting to summarize the net meaning that emerges from dealing with particular facts. Only as general summaries are made from time to time does the mind reach a conclusion or a resting place; and only as conclusions are reached is there an intellectual deposit available in future understanding.

Generalization means capacity for application to the new

III. As the last words indicate, application and generalization lie close together. Mechanical skill for further use may be achieved without any explicit recognition of a principle; nay, in routine and narrow technical matters, conscious formulation may be a hindrance. But without recognition of a principle, without generalization, the power gained cannot be transferred to new and dissimilar matters. The inherent significance of generalization is that it frees a meaning from local restrictions; rather, generalization is meaning so freed; it is meaning emancipated from accidental features so as to be available in new cases. The surest test for detecting a spurious generalization (a statement general in verbal form but not accompanied by discernment of meaning), is the failure of the so-called principle spontaneously to extend itself. The essence of the general is application.

Fossilized versus flexible principles

The true purpose of exercises that apply rules and principles is, then, not so much to drive or drill them in as to give adequate insight into an idea or principle. To treat application as a separate final step is disastrous. In every judgment some meaning is employed as a basis for estimating and interpreting some fact; by this application the meaning is itself enlarged and tested. When the general meaning is regarded as complete in itself, application is treated as an external, non-intellectual use to which, for practical purposes alone, it is advisable to put the meaning. The principle is one self-contained thing; its use is another and independent thing. When this divorce occurs, principles become fossilized and rigid; they lose their inherent vitality, their self-impelling power.

Self-application a mark of genuine principles

A true conception is a moving idea, and it seeks outlet, or application to the interpretation of particulars and the guidance of action, as naturally as water runs downhill. In fine, just as reflective thought requires particular facts of observation and events of action for its origination, so it also requires particular facts and deeds for its own consummation. "Glittering generalities" are inert because they are spurious. Application is as much an intrinsic part of genuine reflective inquiry as is alert observation or reasoning itself. Truly general principles tend to apply themselves. The teacher needs, indeed, to supply conditions favorable to use and exercise; but something is wrong when artificial tasks have arbitrarily to be invented in order to secure application for principles.

Chapter Sixteen

Some General Conclusions

We shall conclude our survey of how we think and how we should think by presenting some factors of thinking which should balance each other, but which constantly tend to become so isolated that they work against each other instead of cooperating to make reflective inquiry efficient.

§ 1. The Unconscious and the Conscious

The understood as the unconsciously assumed

It is significant that one meaning of the term understood is something so thoroughly mastered, so completely agreed upon, as to be assumed; that is to say, taken as a matter of course without explicit statement. The familiar "goes without saying" means "it is understood." If two persons can converse intelligently with each other, it is because a common experience supplies a background of mutual understanding upon which their respective remarks are projected. To dig up and to formulate this common background would be imbecile; it is "understood"; that is, it is silently supplied and implied as the taken-for-granted medium of intelligent exchange of ideas.

Inquiry as conscious formulation

If, however, the two persons find themselves at cross-purposes, it is necessary to dig up and compare the presuppositions, the implied context, on the basis of which each is speaking. The implicit is made explicit; what was unconsciously assumed is exposed to the light of conscious day. In this way, the root of the misunderstanding is removed. Some such rhythm of the unconscious and the conscious is involved in all fruitful thinking. A person in pursuing a consecutive train of thoughts takes some system of ideas for granted (which accordingly he leaves unexpressed, "unconscious") as surely as he does in conversing with others. Some context, some situation, some controlling purpose dominates his explicit ideas so thoroughly that it does not need to be consciously formulated and expounded. Explicit thinking goes on within the limits of what is implied or understood. Yet the fact that reflection originates in a problem makes it necessary at some points consciously to inspect and examine this familiar background. We have to turn upon some unconscious assumption and make it explicit.

Rules cannot be given for attaining a balance

No rules can be laid down for attaining the due balance and rhythm of these two phases of mental life. No ordinance can prescribe at just what point the spontaneous working of some unconscious attitude and habit is to be checked till we have made explicit what is implied in it. No one can tell in detail just how far the analytic inspection and formulation are to be carried. We can say that they must be carried far enough so that the individual will know what he is about and be able to guide his thinking; but in a given case just how far is that? We can say that they must be carried far enough to detect and guard against the source of some false perception or reasoning, and to get a leverage on the investigation; but such statements only restate the original difficulty. Since our reliance must be upon the disposition and tact of the individual in the particular case, there is no test of the success of an education more important than the extent to which it nurtures a type of mind competent to maintain an economical balance of the unconscious and the conscious.

The over-analytic to be avoided

The ways of teaching criticised in the foregoing pages as false "analytic" methods of instruction, all reduce themselves to the mistake of directing explicit attention and formulation to what would work better if left an unconscious attitude and working assumption. To pry into the familiar, the usual, the automatic, simply for the sake of making it conscious, simply for the sake of formulating it, is both an impertinent interference, and a source of boredom. To be forced to dwell consciously upon the accustomed is the essence of ennui; to pursue methods of instruction that have that tendency is deliberately to cultivate lack of interest.

The detection of error, the clinching of truth, demand conscious statement

On the other hand, what has been said in criticism of merely routine forms of skill, what has been said about the importance of having a genuine problem, of introducing the novel, and of reaching a deposit of general meaning weighs on the other side of the scales. It is as fatal to good thinking to fail to make conscious the standing source of some error or failure as it is to pry needlessly into what works smoothly. To over-simplify, to exclude the novel for the sake of prompt skill, to avoid obstacles for the sake of averting errors, is as detrimental as to try to get pupils to formulate everything they know and to state every step of the process employed in getting a result. Where the shoe pinches, analytic examination is indicated. When a topic is to be clinched so that knowledge of it will carry over into an effective resource in further topics, conscious condensation and summarizing are imperative. In the early stage of acquaintance with a subject, a good deal of unconstrained unconscious mental play about it may be permitted, even at the risk of some random experimenting; in the later stages, conscious formulation and review may be encouraged. Projection and reflection, going directly ahead and turning back in scrutiny, should alternate. Unconsciousness gives spontaneity and freshness; consciousness, conviction and control.

§ 2. Process and Product

Play and work again

A like balance in mental life characterizes process and product. We met one important phase of this adjustment in considering play and work. In play, interest centers in activity, without much reference to its outcome. The sequence of deeds, images, emotions, suffices on its own account. In work, the end holds attention and controls the notice given to means. Since the difference is one of direction of interest, the contrast is one of emphasis, not of cleavage. When comparative prominence in consciousness of activity or outcome is transformed into isolation of one from the other, play degenerates into fooling, and work into drudgery.

Play should not be fooling

By "fooling" we understand a series of disconnected temporary overflows of energy dependent upon whim and accident. When all reference to outcome is eliminated from the sequence of ideas and acts that make play, each member of the sequence is cut loose from every other and becomes fantastic, arbitrary, aimless; mere fooling follows. There is some inveterate tendency to fool in children as well as in animals; nor is the tendency wholly evil, for at least it militates against falling into ruts. But when it is excessive in amount, dissipation and disintegration follow; and the only way of preventing this consequence is to make regard for results enter into even the freest play activity.

Nor work, drudgery

Exclusive interest in the result alters work to drudgery. For by drudgery is meant those activities in which the interest in the outcome does not suffuse the means of getting the result. Whenever a piece of work becomes drudgery, the process of doing loses all value for the doer; he cares solely for what is to be had at the end of it. The work itself, the putting forth of energy, is hateful; it is just a necessary evil, since without it some important end would be missed. Now it is a commonplace that in the work of the world many things have to be done the doing of which is not intrinsically very interesting. However, the argument that children should be kept doing drudgery-tasks because thereby they acquire power to be faithful to distasteful duties, is wholly fallacious. Repulsion, shirking, and evasion are the consequences of having the repulsive imposed—not loyal love of duty. Willingness to work for ends by means of acts not naturally attractive is best attained by securing such an appreciation of the value of the end that a sense of its value is transferred to its means of accomplishment. Not interesting in themselves, they borrow interest from the result with which they are associated.

Balance of playfulness and seriousness the intellectual ideal

Free play of mind is normal in childhood

The intellectual harm accruing from divorce of work and play, product and process, is evidenced in the proverb, "All work and no play makes Jack a dull boy." That the obverse is true is perhaps sufficiently signalized in the fact that fooling is so near to foolishness. To be playful and serious at the same time is possible, and it defines the ideal mental condition. Absence of dogmatism and prejudice, presence of intellectual curiosity and flexibility, are manifest in the free play of the mind upon a topic. To give the mind this free play is not to encourage toying with a subject, but is to be interested in the unfolding of the subject on its own account, apart from its subservience to a preconceived belief or habitual aim. Mental play is open-mindedness, faith in the power of thought to preserve its own integrity without external supports and arbitrary restrictions. Hence free mental play involves seriousness, the earnest following of the development of subject-matter. It is incompatible with carelessness or flippancy, for it exacts accurate noting of every result reached in order that every conclusion may be put to further use. What is termed the interest in truth for its own sake is certainly a serious matter, yet this pure interest in truth coincides with love of the free play of thought.

In spite of many appearances to the contrary—usually due to social conditions of either undue superfluity that induces idle fooling or undue economic pressure that compels drudgery—childhood normally realizes the ideal of conjoint free mental play and thoughtfulness. Successful portrayals of children have always made their wistful intentness at least as obvious as their lack of worry for the morrow. To live in the present is compatible with condensation of far-reaching meanings in the present. Such enrichment of the present for its own sake is the just heritage of childhood and the best insurer of future growth. The child forced into premature concern with economic remote results may develop a surprising sharpening of wits in a particular direction, but this precocious specialization is always paid for by later apathy and dullness.

The attitude of the artist

That art originated in play is a common saying. Whether or not the saying is historically correct, it suggests that harmony of mental playfulness and seriousness describes the artistic ideal. When the artist is preoccupied overmuch with means and materials, he may achieve wonderful technique, but not the artistic spirit par excellence. When the animating idea is in excess of the command of method, æsthetic feeling may be indicated, but the art of presentation is too defective to express the feeling thoroughly. When the thought of the end becomes so adequate that it compels translation into the means that embody it, or when attention to means is inspired by recognition of the end they serve, we have the attitude typical of the artist, an attitude that may be displayed in all activities, even though not conventionally designated arts.

The art of the teacher culminates in nurturing this attitude

That teaching is an art and the true teacher an artist is a familiar saying. Now the teacher's own claim to rank as an artist is measured by his ability to foster the attitude of the artist in those who study with him, whether they be youth or little children. Some succeed in arousing enthusiasm, in communicating large ideas, in evoking energy. So far, well; but the final test is whether the stimulus thus given to wider aims succeeds in transforming itself into power, that is to say, into the attention to detail that ensures mastery over means of execution. If not, the zeal flags, the interest dies out, the ideal becomes a clouded memory. Other teachers succeed in training facility, skill, mastery of the technique of subjects. Again it is well—so far. But unless enlargement of mental vision, power of increased discrimination of final values, a sense for ideas—for principles—accompanies this training, forms of skill ready to be put indifferently to any end may be the result. Such modes of technical skill may display themselves, according to circumstances, as cleverness in serving self-interest, as docility in carrying out the purposes of others, or as unimaginative plodding in ruts. To nurture inspiring aim and executive means into harmony with each other is at once the difficulty and the reward of the teacher.

§ 3. The Far and the Near

"Familiarity breeds contempt"

Teachers who have heard that they should avoid matters foreign to pupils' experience, are frequently surprised to find pupils wake up when something beyond their ken is introduced, while they remain apathetic in considering the familiar. In geography, the child upon the plains seems perversely irresponsive to the intellectual charms of his local environment, and fascinated by whatever concerns mountains or the sea. Teachers who have struggled with little avail to extract from pupils essays describing the details of things with which they are well acquainted, sometimes find them eager to write on lofty or imaginary themes. A woman of education, who has recorded her experience as a factory worker, tried retelling Little Women to some factory girls during their working hours. They cared little for it, saying, "Those girls had no more interesting experience than we have," and demanded stories of millionaires and society leaders. A man interested in the mental condition of those engaged in routine labor asked a Scotch girl in a cotton factory what she thought about all day. She replied that as soon as her mind was free from starting the machinery, she married a duke, and their fortunes occupied her for the remainder of the day.

Since only the novel demands attention

Naturally, these incidents are not told in order to encourage methods of teaching that appeal to the sensational, the extraordinary, or the incomprehensible. They are told, however, to enforce the point that the familiar and the near do not excite or repay thought on their own account, but only as they are adjusted to mastering the strange and remote. It is a commonplace of psychology that we do not attend to the old, nor consciously mind that to which we are thoroughly accustomed. For this, there is good reason: to devote attention to the old, when new circumstances are constantly arising to which we should adjust ourselves, would be wasteful and dangerous. Thought must be reserved for the new, the precarious, the problematic. Hence the mental constraint, the sense of being lost, that comes to pupils when they are invited to turn their thoughts upon that with which they are already familiar. The old, the near, the accustomed, is not that to which but that with which we attend; it does not furnish the material of a problem, but of its solution.

Which, in turn, can be given only through the old

The last sentence has brought us to the balancing of new and old, of the far and that close by, involved in reflection. The more remote supplies the stimulus and the motive; the nearer at hand furnishes the point of approach and the available resources. This principle may also be stated in this form: the best thinking occurs when the easy and the difficult are duly proportioned to each other. The easy and the familiar are equivalents, as are the strange and the difficult. Too much that is easy gives no ground for inquiry; too much of the hard renders inquiry hopeless.

The given and the suggested

The necessity of the interaction of the near and the far follows directly from the nature of thinking. Where there is thought, something present suggests and indicates something absent. Accordingly unless the familiar is presented under conditions that are in some respect unusual, it gives no jog to thinking, it makes no demand upon what is not present in order to be understood. And if the subject presented is totally strange, there is no basis upon which it may suggest anything serviceable for its comprehension. When a person first has to do with fractions, for example, they will be wholly baffling so far as they do not signify to him some relation that he has already mastered in dealing with whole numbers. When fractions have become thoroughly familiar, his perception of them acts simply as a signal to do certain things; they are a "substitute sign," to which he can react without thinking. If, nevertheless, the situation as a whole presents something novel and hence uncertain, the entire response is not mechanical, because this mechanical operation is put to use in solving a problem. There is no end to this spiral process: foreign subject-matter transformed through thinking into a familiar possession becomes a resource for judging and assimilating additional foreign subject-matter.

Observation supplies the near, imagination the remote

The need for both imagination and observation in every mental enterprise illustrates another aspect of the same principle. Teachers who have tried object-lessons of the conventional type have usually found that when the lessons were new, pupils were attracted to them as a diversion, but as soon as they became matters of course they were as dull and wearisome as was ever the most mechanical study of mere symbols. Imagination could not play about the objects so as to enrich them. The feeling that instruction in "facts, facts" produces a narrow Gradgrind is justified not because facts in themselves are limiting, but because facts are dealt out as such hard and fast ready-made articles as to leave no room to imagination. Let the facts be presented so as to stimulate imagination, and culture ensues naturally enough. The converse is equally true. The imaginative is not necessarily the imaginary; that is, the unreal. The proper function of imagination is vision of realities that cannot be exhibited under existing conditions of sense-perception. Clear insight into the remote, the absent, the obscure is its aim. History, literature, and geography, the principles of science, nay, even geometry and arithmetic, are full of matters that must be imaginatively realized if they are realized at all. Imagination supplements and deepens observation; only when it turns into the fanciful does it become a substitute for observation and lose logical force.

Experience through communication of others' experience

A final exemplification of the required balance between near and far is found in the relation that obtains between the narrower field of experience realized in an individual's own contact with persons and things, and the wider experience of the race that may become his through communication. Instruction always runs the risk of swamping the pupil's own vital, though narrow, experience under masses of communicated material. The instructor ceases and the teacher begins at the point where communicated matter stimulates into fuller and more significant life that which has entered by the strait and narrow gate of sense-perception and motor activity. Genuine communication involves contagion; its name should not be taken in vain by terming communication that which produces no community of thought and purpose between the child and the race of which he is the heir.